THE EVERYTHING®
LARGE-PRINT
WORD SEARCH BOOK
VOLUME 4

Dear Reader,

"Ready or not, here I come!" You don't have to yell this phrase every time you begin one of these word search puzzles. And counting to twenty with your eyes closed is not required. The words in this book are ready and waiting to play hide-and-seek with you. Children instinctively know that playing helps their brains grow. For adults, studies suggest that playing with puzzles can give our brains a boost. Think of this book as a playground for your mind.

I created these puzzles with large letters for a reason: bigger is better. This format makes it a breeze to scan the grids looking for hidden words. Your word-finding abilities will still be tested, not your vision. Each puzzle has a theme, and I had fun coming up with a variety of topics.

Now, let's play. You're it! With enough dedication, you can round up every word. Happy searching!

Charles Timmerman

Welcome to the EVERYTHING® Series!

These handy, accessible books give you all you need to tackle a difficult project, gain a new hobby, comprehend a fascinating topic, prepare for an exam, or even brush up on something you learned back in school but have since forgotten.

You can choose to read an Everything® book from cover to cover or just pick out the information you want from our four useful boxes: e-questions, e-facts, e-alerts, and e-ssentials. We give you everything you need to know on the subject, but throw in a lot of fun stuff along the way, too.

We now have more than 400 Everything® books in print, spanning such wide-ranging categories as weddings, pregnancy, cooking, music instruction, foreign language, crafts, pets, New Age, and so much more. When you're done reading them all, you can finally say you know Everything®!

PUBLISHER Karen Cooper

MANAGING EDITOR, EVERYTHING® SERIES Lisa Laing

COPY CHIEF Casey Ebert

ACQUISITIONS EDITOR Lisa Laing

EDITORIAL ASSISTANT Matthew Kane

EVERYTHING® SERIES COVER DESIGNER Erin Alexander

LAYOUT DESIGNERS Erin Dawson, Elisabeth Lariviere, Michelle Roy Kelly

THE
EVERYTHING
LARGE-PRINT
WORD SEARCH
BOOK
VOLUME 4

150 all-new word search puzzles—in large print!

Charles Timmerman
Founder of Funster.com

Adams Media
New York London Toronto Sydney New Delhi

Adams Media
An Imprint of Simon & Schuster, Inc.
100 Technology Center Drive
Stoughton, MA 02072

An Everything® Series Book.
Everything® and everything.com® are registered trademarks of Simon & Schuster, Inc.

ADAMS MEDIA and colophon are trademarks of Simon and Schuster.

For information about special discounts for bulk purchases, please contact Simon & Schuster Special Sales at 1-866-506-1949 or business@simonandschuster.com.

The Simon & Schuster Speakers Bureau can bring authors to your live event. For more information or to book an event contact the Simon & Schuster Speakers Bureau at 1-866-248-3049 or visit our website at www.simonspeakers.com.

Manufactured in the United States of America

16 2024

Library of Congress Cataloging-in-Publication Data has been applied for.

ISBN 978-1-4405-3885-8

Acknowledgments

I would like to thank each and every one of the more than half a million people who have visited my website, *www.funster.com*, to play word games and puzzles. You have shown me how much fun puzzles can be and how addictive they can become!

It is a pleasure to acknowledge the folks at Adams Media who made this book possible. I particularly want to thank my editor, Lisa Laing, for so skillfully managing the many projects we have worked on together.

Contents

Introduction

The puzzles in this book are in the traditional word search format. Words in the list are hidden in the grid in any direction: up, down, forward, backward, or diagonally. The words are always found in a straight line, and letters are never skipped. Words can overlap. For example, the letters at the end of the word "MAST" could be used as the start of the word "STERN." Only the letters A to Z are used, and any spaces in an entry are removed. For example, "TROPICAL FISH" would be found in the grid as "TROPICALFISH." All punctuation marks, such as apostrophes and hyphens, are also omitted in the puzzles. Draw a circle around each word that you find in the grid. Then, cross the word off the list so that you will always know what words remain to be found.

A useful strategy is to look for the first letter in a word, then see if the second letter is in any of the eight neighboring letters, and so on until the word is found. Or instead of searching for the first letter in a word, it is sometimes easier to look for letters that standout, like Q, U, X, and Z. Double letters in a word will also stand out and be easier to find in the grid. Another strategy is to simply scan each row, column, and diagonal, looking for any words.

Puzzles

AROMA

BAKING

BROWN

BUTTER

CRUMBS

DARK

EGG

FLOUR

FRENCH

GLUTEN

GRAINS

ITALIAN

JAM

KNEAD

KNIFE

LOAVES

MACHINE

MAKER

MILK

MONEY

NAAN

OIL

OVEN

PAN

PITA

PROTEIN

RAISIN

RISING

ROLLS

RYE

SALT

SLICED

SOFT

SPICE

STARTER

TOASTED

WARM

WHITE

WONDER

YEAST

```
A T I P E D P V G C S N B H
V L S N W O R B R N K Z X N
A A B A A S W A A R D Y V B
U S M I E A W H I T E X K K
A O U A B Y N I N S C K R L
S E R E T R A T S O I W A I
T N C D E T S A O T L N D M
C R G D E K N L M L S G B O
J U N N C X B I L I H U E N
O O S V I L L A E O T Y T E
W L N A P S O N K T R F H Y
A F J R S N I A E I O C B H
R A T O Z H C R V S N R J J
M H V M C G L U T E N G P G
Q E D A E N K Q R G S V S X
N X M N K N I F E G X K H A
```

Solution on Page 314

ADMIRABLE

BEST

BOSS

BRAG

BRILLIANT

CHAMPION

CHOICEST

DESIRABLE

EXCELLENT

EXEMPLARY

EXPERT

EXQUISITE

FABULOUS

FOREMOST

GOOD

GREATEST

INVALUABLE

NOTABLE

OPTIMAL

PEERLESS

PREMIUM

PRICELESS

QUALITY

SELECT

SHINING

SKILLFUL

SPLENDID

STERLING

STRIKING

SUPREME

SURPASSING

WONDERFUL

```
G T S E C I O H C L B E S T
N S T T O H M U I M E R P N
I E R E L B A R I S E D L O
L T I G W S R M V X D O E T
R A K N G O S I P R J O N A
E E I I V A N E L I K G D B
T R N S S A R D L L O M I L
S G G S K T L B E E I N D E
S T V A I N I U S R C A T F
E S O P L E B U A S F I N C
L O P R L L O B E B S U R T
R M T U F L L L O I L S L P
E E I S U E E S U P R E M E
E R M B L C S Q U A L I T Y
P O A H T X X G N I N I H S
U F L E X E M P L A R Y H N
```

Solution on Page 314

BAGELS	MANAGER
BONUS	MEMO
BOSS	MORALE
BREAK	NEW HIRE
BUSINESS	OFFICE
CHAIR	PAGER
CLERK	PARTY
COMPUTER	PAYDAY
COPIER	PENS
DEMOTION	PICTURES
DESK	POSTAGE
DRAWERS	RAISE
EMPLOYER	REPORTS
ERASER	RULER
FIRED	SALARY
FOLDER	SCANNER
GOSSIP	SHELVES
HOLIDAY	STAPLER
INTERNET	
JANITOR	
LAMP	
LAYOFF	

```
P R I A H C O P I E R D X A
K P M A L Y D N S A L A R Y
A C O A T E T K R E L C O A
E O R R S E R U T C I P F D
R M A K R E L P A T S N F Y
B P L N R Y A D I L O H I A
E U E A R N E W H I R E C P
A T S D M E M O T F I R E D
N E I I R E Y O L P M E Q S
R R R P N A M S I S P G C H
E O E A F E W S L E G A B E
D T P G D B S E N A N T E L
L I O E A O O S R N Y S G V
O N R R G N O S E S I O W E
F A T G T U A R S A H P F S
L J S S M S V M R E L U R F
```

Solution on Page 314

AVOCADO

AZTEC

BEANS

BEEF

BURRITO

CARNITAS

CHEESE

CHILI

CILANTRO

CORN

CUISINE

CULTURE

FLAVOR

FOOD

FRESH

GARLIC

GORDITAS

HOT

MAIZE

MASA

MAYAN

MENUDO

MEXICO

MOLE

NATIVE

ONION

PEPPER

PORK

RECIPES

RICE

SALSA

SAUCE

SPANISH

SPICY

SQUASH

TACO

TAMALE

TEQUILA

TOMATO

VARIETY

Mexican Cuisine

```
D O O F T T N N O I N O W S
E R I C E P T A E V I T A N
C T E K S E N I S I U C V A
U A C P Q E B C E T Z A O E
A M H U P F P T A C O R C B
S A I S M E X I C O T N A Y
L L L S E M P U C N I I D R
A E I A A R L I A E R T O A
S V Z S T T F L L F R A T P
C P A I U F I O H L U S A Y
M H I R A C M D A A B P M T
E A E C I M I C R V P A O D
O N Y E Y E Y L O O K N T E
S Q U A S H T C R R G I L Q
G O D U N E M Y O A N S D G
V T Z H L A F P D Q G H O T
```

Solution on Page 314

AMPLIFIER

AUDIO

BUTTONS

CAR

CDS

CHANGER

COMPACT

COMPONENTS

COMPUTER

CORD

DEVICE

DIGITAL

DISC

DVD

EJECT

FEATURES

LASER

LENS

LOADING

MEDIA

MOTOR

MUSIC

OPEN

PAUSE

PLAY

PORTABLE

RADIO

REPEAT

ROTATE

SINGLE

SKIP

SONY

SOUND

SPEAKER

SPIN

STEREO

STOP

TRAY

VIDEO

VOLUME

```
C D S I D B V E S U A P R U
J O T V O L U M E U F O N K
B C O M P A C T D Z T E J E
J B P S R Q F I T O P E L O
F S T N E N O P M O C G R E
W O C I I R E C H A N G E R
F N E P F C U C D I D S V E
N Y J S I O O T S V E I G T
R Q E V L M C B A D D N S S
L R E B P C A R I E I R R C
A D E U M J O G O D F A O Y
S L T K A T I E A I D E M C
E E L B A T R O P I K S Y Y
R N T T A E L S O U N D A P
A S E L R E P E A T F R L L
O F X S F M U S I C T N P D
```

Solution on Page 315

BLOOMING	PUNGENT
BULB	RED
CHIVE	RING
CHOP	ROOT
COOK	ROUND
CRY	SALAD
CUT	SHALLOT
DIP	SKIN
EYES	SLICE
FLAVOR	SOUP
FOOD	STEW
FRIED	STRONG
GARDEN	SWEET
GROW	TEAR
KITCHEN	VIDALIA
LAYERS	WHITE
LEEKS	WILD
ODOR	YELLOW
PEARL	
PEEL	
PLANT	
POWDER	

```
M S T U C W N M M S F S N D
B B J R N P J I Y G U P J A
T H Y C I H T W E T S X C L
O D I D K N Z V L N G T O A
O C X N S P G S A A A T O S
R D H U U N P J Y L R N K D
I S O O O L R A E P D E O E
V F S R P D E I R F E G Z R
Y I T L E E P O S L N N C A
R S D G Y D V N R I E U S E
P E S A P A W I M E H P H T
L Y E L L O W O H P C E B E
B E W F A I O U P C T I U E
N S T O L L A H S I I A L W
Y L K O B G A V H S K C B S
Z R P D L I W W O R G M A Q
```

Solution on Page 315

ACORN	PLANT
ASIA	RED
BARK	ROOT
BED	SHRUB
BIG	SMOKING
BRANCH	SPECIES
CATKINS	SPRING
CUPULE	STRONG
DECIDUOUS	TABLE
DOOR	TALL
FINISH	TANNIN
HARD	TRUNK
HISTORICAL	WATER
LANDSCAPE	WHITE
LARGE	WINE
LEAF	WOOD
LIGHT	
LIMB	
LIVE	
LOG	
NUT	
OLD	

Solution on Page

The Mighty Oak

```
K O F R H Q D X M V J Z L S
T S I O S D O O W H I T E Q
C T N O G R T A B L E V I L
C R I T R T T T N A L P S W
K O S H T E A G C J U B E P
P N H G R Q E N I W P H X I
J G N I K O M S N B U S T N
K P D L S U O U D I C E D Z
N R O C A T K I N S N I G Y
U S O L A S O B R A N C H K
R F R A H T P R E D M E B D
T B A R K B N R I M H P M R
S C U G L Q D J I C A S I A
D B F E P A C S D N A L L H
L L A T P O M E U U G L O F
O F C L A G B T O K X U G R
```

Solution on Page 315

AIRCRAFT

AIRLINE

AIRPORT

BAG

BUS

CAR

CHECK

CLAIM

CLOTHES

DUFFEL

FLIGHT

HANDLE

HEAVY

HOTELS

ITEMS

LABEL

LEATHER

LOCK

LOST

LUGGAGE

PACK

PLANE

PURSE

RAILWAY

ROLLING

SHIP

STORAGE

STYLE

TAG

TICKET

TOTE

TOURIST

TRAIN

TRIP

TRUNK

TSA

UPRIGHT

WEIGHT

WHEELS

ZIPPER

```
Y L B C E S Z L U G G A G E
J O U L A I L E F F U D L P
I S Y N W R L A L S F T A I
J T C H E C K T E D R C B H
S H E P A C K H X O N L E S
Y G P M O A T E P O C A L Q
T I Q L S O Y R G A V I H G
Z E N I L R I A W Y P M U A
S W V C W A I B W F G I B T
Q T F U T R U N K L N G R O
G R O P C S A T H G I L F T
T S I R U O T S R P L A N E
M U A I A A H O T E L S R S
H F R G B G F Z A K O E I R
T D A H W H E E L S R S K U
U B R T I C K E T R A I N P
```

Solution on Page 315

ART
BASKET
BLANKET
CLOTH
COLOR
COTTON
CRAFT
CROCHET
CULTURE
DESIGN
DYE
FABRIC
FIBER
HOBBY
KNIT
KNOT
LACE
LOOM
MILL
NAVAJO
NEEDLE
OVER

PATTERN
PERSIAN
PLAIN
REED
ROPE
RUG
SATIN
SEWING
SHUTTLE
SKILL
STRAW
THREAD
TWILL
UNDER
WEAVER
WEFT
WOMAN
WOOL

```
I L R L O O W K D S R K V U
P L L P L A I N A R T U G L
F I B E R E V A E W K S G L
M K L J M Q N U R E D N N I
B S W O M A N O H Q D K I W
D Y O F V Y N I T A S L W T
D L B A T C L O T H X A E E
E L J B N H N Z U N R H S K
Y O M R O K P T R T C A R N
D V D I S H T E S O W B O A
M E C C U L T U R E A T L L
T R E R E T N C F S T R O B
Z L O R A D J T K O I U C Z
Z J Z P E F J E C A L A S M
E B K R E Y T D E S I G N O
V S M T I Z D J E V N V M T
```

Solution on Page 316

ALE	MEAN
ATTACK	MUSKET
AXE	MUTINY
BATTLE	NASTY
BITE	OCEAN
BOAT	RIFLE
BOOM	ROPE
BULLET	SAIL
CANNON	SCAR
COAST	SHARK
CREW	SHIP
EVIL	SINK
FIERCE	SKULL
FLAIL	SLICE
GOLD	STAB
GROG	SWORD
HOLD	WAVE
HOOK	WOUND
HUNT	
KILLER	
LOOT	
MAST	

```
O N M S X D L R R A L E Y W
Z T J F K B I T E B V B Y K
Z W M A J B X N L I Q G N F
W Q R T C J B U L L E T I B
K A O A K N A H I N A E C O
X P V X A C T Q K O R O P E
X L I E Y A T T A C K S E L
S F M H N N L E E W O H I F
Z R A C S N E F K T E A H I
Z S S V W O Y P T S L R S R
O D T L M N G I W F U K C T
B U S A I L W O U N D M A G
N A S T Y C R D L O H O R S
S K U L L D E A O D B O F I
U M A B G T N K O D G B O N
N V B O I E B A T S R O L K
```

Solution on Page 316

ANTIQUE	NOTES
BIG	OFFICE
BOOK	PEN
CHAIR	PHONE
COMPUTER	READ
CORNER	SCHOOL
DEN	SEAT
DRAW	SIT
EXECUTIVE	SMALL
FRENCH	STAND
FURNITURE	STUDY
HEAVY	SUPPLIES
HELP	SURFACE
HOME	TOP
INK	WALL
KEYBOARD	WOOD
LAP	WORK
LEG	WRITE
LIGHT	
LOCK	
METAL	
MOUSE	

```
M D G D B P U L M L Z W P G
W I R E H V E P O T O O H I
F D D P L G V L U C K O O B
E F N L O O H C S X K D N T
O Y A O F F I C E Y V A E H
L M T N I N O O N N W X W G
S A S O K R F M E E E A U I
S Y T T N N U P Q C R D L L
Y K W E I G R U U D L F H L
L T R S M A N T I Q U E F C
X I I O D E I E C A F R U S
N S T A W V T R I A H C K T
V E E A E S U P P L I E S U
R R P A L T R L A X S A P D
B U S L T K E Y B O A R D Y
H I F Q X H O M E I E Z U P
```

Solution on Page 316

ABSORB	LINEN
BAR	MOISTURE
BEACH	NAPKIN
BLOT	PAPER
CLEAN	POOL
CLOTH	RACK
COLOR	RAYON
COTTON	RUBBING
DECORATIVE	SOAP
DESIGN	SOFT
DISH	SPA
DRY	SWIM
FABRIC	TEA
FACE	WASH
FIBERS	WET
FOLDED	WIPE
GUEST	WOVEN
GYM	WRAP
HAIR	
HAND	
HOT	
KITCHEN	

```
M G Y L D N A H N M D E Z X
F R E X N I K P A N L M W S
C R G V G D I C E I R T E O
T V T M I W S Z L E R W U Z
J T O S S T D R C O E A Q U
O S H W E E A F E B T S P A
R E Q K D B W R A P L H Z E
Q U G L I C U N O T T O C T
C G O H U T O P B C N P T N
R F N B S Y C A R S E H P R
F G D I A A B H R J S D O E
U Y O R B L N E E O F L O P
V M A S Y B B F A N O I L A
X C O O L I U P A C T N X P
K R I F F A B R I C H E W H
B N F T E P I W O V E N W Z
```

Solution on Page 316

ALIGN

ANCIENT

ANNULAR

BLINDING

BLOCK

BRIGHT

CHASERS

CORONA

COVER

CYCLE

DAY

EARTH

ECLIPSE

EVENT

FULL

GLASSES

LUNAR

MOON

NATURAL

NIGHT

OBSCURE

OMEN

ORBIT

PARTIAL

PATH

PINHOLE

PLANET

RARE

RING

SCIENCE

SHADOW

SKY

SOLAR

SPACE

STAR

SUN

TOTAL

UMBRA

VIEW

VISIBLE

```
L L P Y Z O X W E I V T R I
N T B R A L O S O H O H J S
O I K Y J D H N A T N T P Y
O B G R A T R N A A A A I K
M R V H R A O L T N C P N C
B O S A T R A U N E V E H O
Y R E S O I R U O C M A O L
O K S C T A L G Y O S G L B
W X S R L A N C I E N T E U
B W A N R I L B R I G H T A
S P L T D E P S R C O V E R
H D G N N O B S C U R E N B
A L I G N E C N E I C S A M
E L B I S I V S R A N U L U
B U D Q R A R E L W V U P A
P F D C C F V E Y I O X S B
```

Solution on Page 317

ARCADE

ATM

BAGS

BOOKS

BROWSE

BUSY

CANDY

CARS

CASHIER

CHARGE

CINEMA

CLERKS

COFFEE

COMPARE

COOKIES

COUPONS

CROWDS

DEALS

DOORS

DRINKS

EXIT

FAMILY

FASHION

FRIENDS

HANGOUT

JEWELRY

KIDS

KIOSKS

LAYAWAY

LINES

MONEY

MOVIES

NOISE

PEOPLE

PERFUME

PRICE

REFUND

RETAIL

RETURNS

STAIRS

Shopping Complex

```
T U Y Z S K O O B D O O R S
I B Y L R Y U L R E F U N D
X W S N I E D H A N G O U T
E L E S A M E N C Y I G S Q
C I I C T U A B A H A T M X
I A K O S F L F S C S W Q M
R T O U W R S A H J E S A P
P E O P L E F R I E N D S Y
D R C O M P A R E W I I K P
A M E N I C E E R E L K I H
C B U S Y H D T S L C M O S
E L B C I A R U B R O W S E
K B E A C O I R A Y F R K I
C H A R G E N N F F F Z S V
A I A S K S K S K J E Z R O
C R O W D S S S M O N E Y Z M
```

Solution on Page 317

ACE

ANDRE AGASSI

ARTHUR ASHE

BOBBY RIGGS

BORIS BECKER

CLAY

COURT

DAVIS CUP

DEUCE

DROP SHOT

FAULT

GAME

JIMMY CONNORS

JOHN MCENROE

LET

LOVE

MARTINA HINGIS

MATCH

MICHAEL CHANG

NET

PASSING SHOT

PETE SAMPRAS

RAFAEL NADAL

ROGER FEDERER

ROLAND GARROS

SERVE

SMASH

SPIN

STEFAN EDBERG

US OPEN

WILD CARDS

```
S T E F A N E D B E R G A L
E H S A M S W L C U N R R C
R T B U A C E U S A T S J R
V J O L R T E O H H D I E O
E B R T T D P C U R M R S L
E O I F I E L R A M E N A A
O B S K N E A C Y D E N R N
R B B Z A S D C E T D D P D
N Y E H H L O F P R L R M G
E R C E I N R U E U O O A A
C I K W N E C A E O V P S R
M G E O G S G L M C E S E R
N G R O I A I M A T C H T O
H S R V S P I N G Y T O E S
O P A S S I N G S H O T P Z
J D I R A F A E L N A D A L
```

Solution on Page 317

ABSORB

AERATING

AERIAL

ANCHOR

BASE

BEET

BOTANY

BULB

CARROT

CROPS

DEEP

DIG

ECOLOGY

FLOWER

FOOD

FOREST

GARDEN

GROW

HAIR

HERB

ONION

ORGAN

PARSNIP

PLANT

POTATO

RUTABAGA

SHOOT

SOIL

STORAGE

SUPPORT

SURFACE

TAPROOT

TEA

THICK

TOOTH

TREE

TUBER

TURNIP

WEED

YAM

```
G Q A W P A C Y D C R O P S
T M E U E N C R I A H N L D
V E N R H C D Q B R O M A R
D B I K A H H S K R O Z N T
K A L D G O O E G O T Y T R
L C E U A R E A R T A N K E
E E I R B G N D E B T A X E
P C E H A E S A B I O T C L
L K A R T T P S U P P O R T
K I O F U A I H T B L B O F
H T O B R M X N T O W O T G
S N U S E U A G G O R O A M
D O N Z W E S Y R P O R D O
O I F O O D T G A H D T E A
P N J E L C I T S E R O F W
A O V R F D P I N R U T Q O
```

Solution on Page 317

ACTOR

ATHLETE

ATTENTION

AUDIENCE

AUTOGRAPH

BAND

BASEBALL

CHEER

CLUB

CRUSH

CULT

DESIRE

DEVOTED

EVENT

FAMOUS

FANATIC

FANDOM

FANZINE

FOLLOW

GROUP

HERO

IDOL

INTENSE

INTEREST

LIKE

LOVE

LOYAL

MAIL

MOVIES

MUSIC

PATRON

PLAYER

POLITICS

SINGER

SPORT

STAR

SUPPORT

TEAM

WEBSITE

WORSHIP

Solution on Page

```
B M S T A R P L A Y E R R C
S B G M C I E A L O Y A L U
W A A R A R P G T R O P S L
H N W S O T U O N R P E P T
Y D E A E U H S L I O C M R
I T B F G B P L H I S N U O
D E S I R E A S E M T E S P
O W I E W V R L U T V I I P
L O T E R O G K L O E D C U
K L E S W E O D L B M U F S
M L L N O I T N E T T A D E
X O R E H L U N Q V N Z F I
X F D T L I A M I A O Q M V
E V E N T K A C T O R T A O
X U I I A E N I Z N A F E M
B U L C D F C H E E R R T D
```

Solution on Page 318

BLOUSE

BOARD

BURN

CLOTH

COLLAR

COTTON

CREASES

DRY

ELECTRIC

FABRIC

FLAT

FOLD

FORMAL

HEAT

HOT

IRON

JACKET

MAID

MATERIAL

METAL

MIST

PANTS

PRESS

SHIRT

SILK

SKIRT

SLACKS

SMOOTH

SPRAY

STARCH

STEAM

STRAIGHT

SUIT

TAILOR

TIES

TOOL

TROUSERS

WATER

WORK

WRINKLE

```
I A T I U S K C A L S L Q M
X T N T S C I K C H R A J T
J R S O V U L A I R E T A M
M I L Y R D C O R H S E C B
M K T H G I A R T S U M K D
T S S E R P H O C H O T E I
A P J B F E O E E A R I T A
H I A D L M T I L S T E A M
E F L R S A D T E K B S E R
G T C A X A M S D W N H H E
D L C O L L A R L H X I C T
D J S B T E S U O L B R R A
V Q I A R T N L F F T T A W
Y X L C N R O L I A T L T O
D F K A U O U N Y A R P S R
D R P B T I Z F A R S V S K
```

Solution on Page 318

AARON	HALEY
AIDAN	ISAAC
ALEXIS	JACK
ALYSSA	JAMES
ANDREW	JASON
ANGEL	JOHN
ANNA	JULIA
ASHLEY	KAYLA
AVA	KEVIN
BROOKE	KYLIE
CALEB	LOGAN
CHLOE	LUKE
CONNOR	MARIA
DANIEL	NOAH
DYLAN	PAIGE
ELIJAH	RYAN
ELLA	SARAH
EMILY	TYLER
EMMA	
ETHAN	
EVAN	
GRACE	

Common First Names

```
Z G A L E X I S P H H C W L
F T M S A I A A R O N E U N
J A M E S J D V O T R K T Y
U A J A H Y A A N D E O L Q
L M A Y L A L S N N H O J K
I C A L E B J A O I O R S Z
A Z I I Y E D I C N E B Y A
V R D M K I E L L A O L C J
Y E L E A J K E Y E L A H F
M L T U Y M G I O J H N H F
Z Y H H L N A L Y D C N C N
S T G R A C E Y O R Y A N A
B K E V I N G K E G J J M V
B U P K A R I A I R A M I E
D O R S A R A H Q C E N G C
Z Q V C H R P B K G W H A K
```

Solution on Page 318

ABANDONED

AISLE

BASKET

BROKEN

CARRY

CHECKOUT

CHILDREN

COLLECT

COUNTER

FOLDING

FOOD

FULL

GOODS

GROCERY

HANDLE

ITEMS

LINE

LOAD

MALL

MARKET

METAL

PARKING

PLASTIC

PUSH

RETAIL

RETRIEVAL

RETURN

RIDE

ROLL

SEAT

SHOP

SQUEAK

STEEL

STORE

SWIVEL

TRANSPORT

WAGON

WALK

WHEEL

WIRE

```
W I R E N M G N I K R A P W
W A G O N R O L L U A M O R
A T K O O T E K S A B E H K
L E A C O U N T E R L T S H
K K E V I D U R R N I A E H
I R U M H O S O D I N L T G
Y A Q M K O B P Z L E E A N
P M S C C I T S A L P V B I
S M E T I V C N L A Y I A D
A H A N D L E A L M R W N L
C I T S O R L R U I R S D O
L K S A D W L T F L A C O F
I E D L B R O K E N C T N Q
E D I R E H C E N R U T E R
W H E E L S T O R E H E D R
C L U Y H S U P S D O O F I
```

Solution on Page 318

BELT

BLACK

BOYS

BUTTON

CASUAL

CLOTH

COTTON

CREASE

CUFF

DENIM

DESIGN

DOCKERS

DRESS

FABRIC

FLY

FORMAL

HEM

HIP

INSEAM

IRON

JEANS

KHAKIS

KNICKERS

LEG

LONG

MATERIAL

MEN

PANTS

POCKET

PRESS

SHORTS

SILK

SIZE

SLACKS

SUIT

TAILOR

WAIST

WOOL

WORK

ZIPPER

```
U Y F P Z S J T B N I W J S
F V A K L I S S C Q O M E W
J W S O E Z I I P R E S S I
N W P U G E R A K H L F L Y
D U A L I B O W T A I L O R
N W N V A T N O C Y H Q N E
I J T F E U L K B H N K G P
O D S K S C S M W O A E I P
N R C R S M W A T S Y H M I
D O C K E R S T C T E S C Z
P B T H R K U E U R D S M O
X L I T D B C R M O E N A P
L A M R O F R I I H S A E T
O C U F F C Q A N S I E S L
O K K T H H L L E K G J N E
W A A W R P E Q D U N G I B
```

Solution on Page 319

BOX

CARDS

CHANCE

CHESS

CHILDREN

CLUE

COUNTERS

DICE

FAMILY

FRIENDS

FUN

GAME

KIDS

LEARN

LIFE

LOSE

LUCK

MARBLES

MARKER

MONOPOLY

MOVES

PIECES

PLAY

POINTS

POPULAR

RISK

ROLL

RULES

SCENARIO

SCRABBLE

SORRY

SPACES

SPIN

SQUARE

TABLE

TIMER

TOKENS

TRIVIA

TURN

WIN

```
U A C B T X B R U L E S D P
N I W H L I S S E V O M L L
N V Y P E N M A F U N R U T
P I E C E S R E T N U O C G
O R P K I N S Y R D P H K Y
I T O S S C E N A R I O F B
N T G X H F T A B L E S R Y
T S P A C E S O D D P E I R
S O N M M S C R A B B L E R
R C V R O E E A I S E B N O
E F I L K N N L Q C A R D S
K U R D K Q O U E I X A S U
R E L I G O A P S I O M G O
A O D C S R Q O O O B B A V
M S L E E K T P L L Q Q U L
K S M L L F A M I L Y S F T
```

Solution on Page 319

AIRBRUSH

ART

ATHLETIC

BLACK

BRAND

CASUAL

CLOTHES

COLOR

CONCERT

DESIGN

FABRIC

GRAPHIC

GYM

HANES

HUMOR

JEANS

JERSEY

LOGO

LONG

MESSAGES

NECK

PICTURE

PLAIN

POCKET

PRINT

SHIRT

SIZE

SLEEVE

SOFT

SPORT

STYLE

SUMMER

TAG

TEE

THIN

TOP

UNDER

UNIFORM

WIT

WORN

```
X U N D E R S N A E J P U F
F A V A V J V A G Y P S O H
C O N C E R T A K I D T M T
A F P E E H T R C N S Y E I
S A J M L S U T A F P E Y W
U B T E S U U R L P R S D K
A R T S K R B S B L I R U G
L I T S E B V J H A N E S Z
C C F A T R M G P I T J G M
L L O G O I R P R N R N Y V
O R S E U A O E O A O T M E
T O R S P C F K M L P E K E
H L S H K A I T U M S Z V E
E O I E C I N I H T U I V H
S C T U E V U E L Y T S T H
R W O R N W B W M H F Z V S
```

Solution on Page 319

ANCHOR

BARGE

BOATS

BRIDGE

CAPTAIN

CREW

CRUISE

DECK

DESTROYER

DOCK

ENGINES

FISHING

FRIGATE

GALLEY

HARBOR

HULL

KEEL

LAKES

LINER

MARITIME

MAST

MERCHANT

MILITARY

MOTOR

OCEAN

POWER

RIVERS

RUDDER

SAILORS

SEAS

SINK

SLOOP

STERN

SUBMARINE

TANKER

TRAVEL

TURBINE

VESSELS

WATER

YACHT

```
O K N A E C O C D F G P K T
Y S R O L I A S I R N O N T
E R O B R A H P V I I W I S
G R A F D M C D T G H E S A
D E S T R O Y E R A S R Y M
I D R U I B C C S T I E T O
R D I W B L I K W E F N A T
B U V I E M I T I R A M N O
W R E E X R A M T H E S K R
A T R N S N C R C S K S E E
T Z S T C S A R I G E E R N
E Y A H L V E U A N N I E I
R O O O E M R L I S E K A L
B R O L T C L G S T E R N L
P P M U B E N I B R U T Q U
T H C A Y E G R A B O Q C H
```

Solution on Page 319

ARCHERY

AUTO RACING

BADMINTON

BASEBALL

BASKETBALL

BOATING

BOWLING

CHEERLEADING

CRICKET

CURLING

CYCLING

DANCE

EQUESTRIAN

FENCING

FISHING

FOOTBALL

GOLF

GYMNASTICS

HOCKEY

HORSE RACING

JUDO

LACROSSE

ROWING

RUGBY

RUNNING

SHOOTING

SOCCER

SOFTBALL

SWIMMING

TRIATHLON

VOLLEYBALL

WRESTLING

```
O L A C R O S S E C N A D O
D L B T S C I T S A N M Y G
U A A R C H E R Y B G U R N
J B E Q U E S T R I A N E I
G T M W R E S T L I N G U M
N F N I G R B O A T I N G M
I O O G N L L A B T O O F I
N S T N I E T F A K B L G W
N G N I C A R E S R O H N S
U N I T A D H N K E W T I G
R I M O R I O C E C L A L N
O L D O O N C I T C I I C I
W R A H T G K N B O N R Y H
I U B S U K E G A S G T C S
N C L L A B Y E L L O V S I
G P B A S E B A L L G O L F
```

Solution on Page 320

ACTION

ACTRESS

AWARDS

BOMB

CAMERAS

COLOR

COMEDY

CRITICS

CUT

DOUBLES

DRAMA

DUBBING

EDITOR

EXTRAS

FANS

FEATURE

FLOP

FRAMES

GAFFERS

GENRE

HIT

HORROR

LEADS

LIGHTS

LOOPING

MAKEUP

MUSICAL

MYSTERY

OSCAR

PARTY

PLOT

POPCORN

PROPS

RATINGS

SCRIPT

SEQUEL

STARS

STUNTS

THEME

TICKET

Silver Screen

```
L E U Q E S L G S B H J S S
E S H J D I P N T R C N R P
X I O R G O A I A O R J L R
T R A H P F U B R T I O C O
R W T C E O C B S I T Z R P
A S O O T R T U L D I M A S
S R G E G W U D N E C U C T
N N F N N A C T R E S S S U
T E K C I T F A A C T I O N
A F L O P T W F M E L C Y T
E M W N O H A N E E F A R S
M R A B O M B R P R R L E D
E O N R L F R A M E S A T A
H L R E D Y R T P I R C S E
T O V R G T N C O M E D Y L
R C X E Y R C P U E K A M Y
```

Solution on Page 320

ALASKA

ANIMAL

AQUARIUM

AQUATIC

BEACH

BROWN

CARNIVORA

CLAMS

CUTE

DIURNAL

DIVE

FISH

FLOAT

FORAGE

FUR

HABITAT

HUNTED

KELP

KEYSTONE

MAMMAL

MARINE

OCEAN

PACIFIC

PAWS

PELT

PREY

PUP

ROCKS

SEA

SHARK

SHORE

SKIN

SLIPPERY

SMALL

SPECIES

SWIM

TAIL

WATER

WHISKERS

ZOO

```
C B X N L O S Q J N E W J R
D O C O B E W F X C U T E K
L O N L C D I U R N A L N R
I Z I L A M M A M K Q M I A
A F K A R M K A E F U W R H
T S S M N V S Y W I A C A S
L H L S I L S A R S T B M O
E V I D V T T A A H I E A S
P U P S O E U S L T C O N K
W K P N R Q P P A C I F I C
P R E Y A E L T S N E Q M O
J C R L C M K E K G W N A R
K U Y I P T A S A T A O L F
F D E T N U H R I E H J R S
P S H O R E O Q C H C A E B
D M O V R F D O P A W S K Y
```

Solution on Page 320

AXLE	RIDE
BALANCE	SADDLE
CARNIVAL	SAFETY
CHAIN	SEAT
CIRCUS	SHOW
CLOWNS	SINGLE
CRANK	SKILL
CYCLE	SPOKE
FALL	STUNT
FESTIVAL	TALL
FRAME	TIRE
FUN	TOY
GIRAFFE	TRAINING
HEIGHT	TRICK
HELMET	UNSTABLE
HOBBY	UPRIGHT
JUGGLE	VEHICLE
LEGS	WHEEL
MUNI	
PARADE	
PEDAL	
PRACTICE	

Unicycle

```
Z S S H O W F U W Y P T W Y
Y Z G E T R I C K O M N I R
B T N E A T H G I R P U Z F
B H E M L T I N U M L F C Y
O S E F F A R I G A K H Y S
H T D I A D V N V A A S C S
K U A Q G S F I Q I U U L L
S N R L L H T A N N P C E L
P T A Z L S T R S R M R L A
O E P R E B R T A R A I J F
K O D F C I A C E E K C U G
E Y S A D B T L L S A R G C
W H E E L I D G A I P X G C
Y V R E C D N Y S N W O L C
Z B I E A I V E H I C L E E
D L T S S Y O T E M L E H G
```

Solution on Page 320

APOGEE	PLANET
AXIS	PLUTO
CIRCLE	PULL
COMET	RADIUS
CURVE	REVOLVE
CYCLE	RING
DEBRIS	ROCKET
ELLIPSE	ROTATE
FOLLOW	ROUND
FORCE	SOLAR
GRAVITY	SPACE
JUPITER	SPHERE
KEPLER	STAR
MARS	SUN
MOON	SYSTEM
MOTION	TRACK
MOVE	VENUS
NEPTUNE	YEAR
NEWTON	
PATH	
PERIOD	
PHYSICS	

```
A M D S S I X A F Y M P J E
E B R P T U L K E T E M O C
S A A Q I D N U O R T O S R
M C D P Y J Z J I I S V P O
E W I F O L L O W N Y E H F
W J U M L G D T H G S H E K
V G S S L N E L C R I C R R
X D N C U R V E N U T P E N
D E S O P N S R E V O L V E
O B P C I P E Z Q Q P R T W
G R A V I T Y V C E T A R T
Y I P L I S O E K Y T T O O
H S L P Y O Y M A O C S C N
L E U P G L V H R R K L K D
G J T K C A R T P L A N E T
Z N O O M R M X K C P A T H
```

Solution on Page 321

ACES

ANACONDA

BET

BILLABONG

CALL

CARD

CASINO

CHIPS

COMMUNITY

DEAL

DECK

DEUCES

DOUBLE

DRAW

FIVE

FLUSH

GAME

GUTS

HAND

HIGH

HOLD

KING

KUHN

LOW

MIXED

OMAHA

OXFORD

PAIR

PASS

PLAY

POT

QUEEN

RAZZ

ROYAL

SHUFFLE

SPLIT

STUD

TABLE

TEXAS

WIN

Solution on Page 304

Poker Games

```
B W Y K L B C D R O F X O M
Y I A W L D E D T H D I C Q
E N L W A U P D D L O H A A
T O P L C L A X U F A N C K
S R E E A A S Y J T A E C M
V D S P L B S T Z C S E D G
U G T A N F O I O G D U Q C
N E Y E S N F N N W N Q H J
D O M I X E D U G O S I U V
R R A Z Z A O M H L P E K Z
A H A N D C S M D S L G T X
C Y V W Y T Z O A B I D E H
V W N H U K U C A H T M B M
M I D G S B U T R I A P Q B
I A W F L U S H I G H G N V
O N W E V I F W V N W W W K
```

Solution on Page 321

BASEBALL

BEACH TOYS

BICYCLES

BOATS

CARD GAMES

CHECKERS

COLLECTIBLE

COMPUTERS

CRAFTS

CRAYONS

DOLLS

EDUCATIONAL

ELECTRONICS

FUN

GADGETS

GUITAR

ICE SKATES

IPOD

JACKS

KITES

LEGOS

MODEL CAR

MONOPOLY

MOTORCYCLES

NINTENDO

PIANO

PLAYSTATION

RADIO

SCOOTER

SKIS

TRAINS

VIDEO GAMES

VOLLEYBALL

WATER GUNS

XBOX

```
R S N U G R E T A W X B O X
A S O G E L L A B E S A B Y
T B V O L L E Y B A L L D L
I M O T O R C Y C L E S O O
U S C S R E T U P M O C L P
G K Y C O W R A D I O R L O
V B G O S D O R Z L Z A S N
C I A O T N N S L F Y Y C O
H C D T V H I E K S U O R M
E Y G E D U C A T I O N A L
C C E R O T S A R N S S F R
K L T M I G T S E T I K T S
E E S B P I A N O B H N S K
R S L H O S E M A G D R A C
S E S N D M O D E L C A R A
B O A T S E T A K S E C I J
```

Solution on Page 321

AQUATIC	LIVING
BAT	MINERALS
CAVERN	MOUNTAIN
CAVING	NATURE
CLIFF	OPENING
COLD	PASSAGE
COOL	PIT
DAMP	ROCK
DANK	ROOM
DARK	SEA
DEN	SHAFT
DOLOMITE	SHELTER
DRAWINGS	SPACE
ENTRANCE	STONE
EROSION	STREAM
EXPLORE	SURFACE
FRACTURE	TUNNEL
GEOLOGY	WATER
GLACIER	
GROTTO	
HOLE	
LARGE	

```
D N O L C C M D A D P F J L
C A Q U A T I C L I F F P O
O S N V V S N A T U R E O W
L P E K I H E W N E E L O H
D R E K N A R I Q N T R E W
N D R N G F A G E O L O G Y
G A O K I T L H C T E O A W
D N S L N N S F N S H M S S
T L I U O P G R A X S B S S
I U O V A M N A R O R X A U
L M N C I Q I C T N E D P R
K A E N Z L W T N K I J M F
E E R B E A A U E I C C A A
R R A G T L R R S E A O D C
C T M E E N D E X P L O R E
W S R H Q O T T O R G L W E
```

Solution on Page 321

ARCHITECT	JUDGE
ARTIST	LAWYER
ASTRONAUT	MANAGER
AUTHOR	MARKETING
BAKER	MECHANIC
BIOLOGIST	MUSICIAN
BUTCHER	NURSE
CAPTAIN	PAINTER
CARPENTER	PILOT
CASHIER	POSTMAN
CHEMIST	SURGEON
COACH	TAILOR
COUNSELOR	WAITRESS
DENTIST	
DIETITIAN	
DOCTOR	
DRAFTSMAN	
ECONOMIST	
EDITOR	
GEOLOGIST	
HISTORIAN	
JANITOR	

```
H S R O T C O D E N T I S T
C U A G E O L O G I S T B E
A R R E R O T I N A J S U S
O G T D R O L I A T E I T R
C E I I R G J W I P G M C U
P O S T M A N A R A D O H N
R N T O C U F I O C U N E A
E T C R A T B T T N J O R I
T U A M S H I R S E C C E C
N A R E H O O E I M K E Y I
I I N P C I R L S H R A R W S
A O E H E O O S T X E N A U
P R N A R E G A N A M K L M
Z T T N Q D I E T I T I A N
O S E I X T S I M E H C P B
U A R C H I T E C T O L I P
```

Solution on Page 322

ALKALI

ALLOY

BRONZE

BUILDING

CAN

CHEMISTRY

COINS

COMPOUND

COPPER

ELECTRONS

ELEMENT

EXPENSIVE

FERROUS

GOLD

GRAY

HARD

HEAT

IONS

IRON

JEWELRY

LEAD

MAGNET

MATERIAL

MELT

MINES

NICKEL

ORE

PAN

PRECIOUS

RARE

RUST

SCREW

SHINY

SILVER

SODIUM

STAINLESS

STEEL

STRENGTH

TIN

ZINC

Solution on

```
N A P T C R Y A R G K G K K
Z I S N O I R U O L E A D J
I B C K P A L K A L I N T T
G U H K P R E C I O U S S N
M I F A E T W W L O B T U E
I L E Z R L E P P E A I R M
N D R S C D J M X I E N A E
E I R C P H O P N B M T A L
S N O R T C E L E D E H S E
N G U E O N E M J R L T D Z
I R S W S S G G I M T G A N
O A O I S F O A U S M N L O
C R V R E V L I S Z T E L R
E E H O H P D D X I A R O B
V C A N S O M A G N E T Y S
D X I K S H I N Y C H S B D
```

Solution on Page 322

AMUSED

BEAM

BRACES

CAMERA

CHEEKS

CHILDREN

CONTENT

CREASE

DENTIST

DIMPLE

EYES

FACE

FAKE

FEELINGS

FLASH

FLIRT

FRIENDLY

FUN

GLAD

GOOD

GREETING

GRIN

HAPPY

HUMOR

JOY

KIND

LAUGH

LIPS

LOVE

MOUTH

MUSCLE

PEOPLE

PHOTO

PICTURE

PLAY

PLEASED

PRETTY

SMIRK

SOCIAL

TEETH

Solution on Page

```
E O R D G F R P H U M O R K
X C E G R I N W B S I G T N
N F L I R T G O O D A Y N U
I A P I C T U R E V O L U H
D H O P L E A S E D J D F Y
J M E D H B R A C E S N K D
O O P I E G N C O N T E N T
Y U H M B N U S C C S I A M
K T O P K G T A H R K R N B
N H T L S G N I L E E F A G
H A O E A E L H S M E A F M
A T C Z R D L A A T H P S A
M A E S R P S C I P C L P E
F P D E S U M A S C P A I B
W W N Y T L V L X U O Y L X
D Y O E K A F K R I M S A J
```

Solution on Page 322

AMISH	OPEN
AUTO	PARK
AXLE	PEOPLE
BABY	PULL
BUGGY	QUEEN
CAR	RIDE
CHARIOT	ROAD
COACH	ROYAL
COMFORT	SEAT
COVERED	SURREY
DOOR	TOUR
DRIVER	TRAVEL
ELEGANCE	VEHICLE
ENCLOSED	WAGON
FOOTMAN	WEDDING
HARNESS	WHEEL
HOOD	WHIP
HORSE	WINDOW
JOURNEY	
KING	
LEATHER	
OMNIBUS	

```
H Y R T N E E U Q K O X L E
O C O I P N B S R K O T L L
F U A J S S E N R A H R U X
R R D O O R E O A O C O P A
W E Q U C P N G S M H F Q E
E V H C R O G C A U Q T M U G
M T E N K M L W R E T O K C
V A K E A T O I R A H C O N
G E W Y L G S F E M R V M F
G L H O H L E S Y T E S N B
W X U I D O D L P R V E I A
W H I P C N O B E A I F B B
P N S G E L I D O V R B U Y
A G N I D D E W P E D G S G
R I M Y M S I U L L G K G G
K L R O Y A L R E Y P Y Q P
```

Solution on Page 322

ADDICTING

ARCADE

ATARI

BLOCK

BUILD

CLASSIC

CLEAR

COLOR

COMPUTER

CONSOLE

DESIGN

DROP

FIT

FUN

GAME

GRAVITY

LEVEL

LINE

MATRIX

MUSIC

NINTENDO

PIECES

PLAY

POLYOMINOES

POPULAR

PUZZLE

ROTATE

ROWS

RUSSIA

SCORE

SHAPE

SOVIET

SPEED

SPIN

SQUARE

STACK

STRATEGY

TETROMINOES

VIDEO

```
N D L Q O E D I V E G P F Y
A S H A P E L Z Z U P T I V
K C A T S D T S O V I E T H
L F C I M A T R I X G T W P
G U G U O C S S Q U A R E L
N N S C K R E T U P M O C A
W I R C D A T A R I E M X Y
C E O I R A D D I C T I N G
U L W S O D N E T N I N I E
B P S S P M Q Y P E P O P T
U O R A E L C T A L I E S A
I P O L Y O M I N O E S P R
L U T C T L S V N S C V E T
D L A W I S H A Y N E M E S
Q A T N U U M R I O S F D L
E R E R O C S G V C O L O R
```

Solution on Page 323

AGING

ALE

AMOUNT

BEER

BOURBON

BREWERY

BROWN

CASK

COOPER

CRATE

FISH

FLAVOR

FOOD

FUEL

GAS

GUN

HOLLOW

HOOP

KEG

LARGE

LID

OAK

OIL

PICKLE

PLASTIC

PORK

RAIN

RANCH

RIM

ROLL

ROUND

RUM

SHIP

STORE

TAP

UNIT

VESSEL

WATER

WINE

WOOD

```
X Z P C P Q A V D V G M G Y
R S L L O O H O T E L A R G
I F L B D O O F B S W E S Y
E B O G L W P H O S W O H W
K R R L A R G E U E I K I M
P O O G C I T O R L G A P T
O W U R A I N B B O G O I D
R N N N Y H T D O I V N C H
K T D Y C N T S N T U A K S
B S Y N U F Q G A E J U L I
Y C A O K U E P Y L Z R E F
M R M C D K E W G M P R U B
H A I K N C H I A T O E R M
O T I M Q D C N S T L E Y K
Y E N L L B P E S K E I I K
J P F U U B B Y T B H R D W
```

Solution on Page 323

BIG

BOVINE

BULL

CART

CATTLE

CLOVEN

DRAFT

DRIVER

FARM

HAUL

HOOF

HORN

LARGE

LOAD

LOGGING

MALE

OXEN

PAIR

PLOW

POWER

PULL

RANCH

RIDING

SHOEING

STEER

STRENGTH

STRONG

TAIL

TEAM

TILL

TRAIL

WAGON

WHIP

WHOA

WORK

YOKE

```
C Y G D G H L C J D B M O C
A L N R N N F O A I G Z A M
E D O I T A I L G T W R R B
J B R V S T R E N G T H U C
A G T E E N I V O B I L I Y
L J S R A N C H L H L N E P
C U F W E R L L I T S E G N
L Y A O H W E P A I R E N Q
H D O R B A O E R H L G I I
H Y S K Q G L P T F A R D M
T T Q M E O P H L S P A I M
O N U D A N E X O L H L R L
D X T D P L R I E O U A O L
P U P K M A E T R A F P V W
N L N L B Z K N H X D E P F
C Z X Z F W R C L A N T S A
```

BARBECUE

BENCH

BIKERS

BLANKET

CANOE

CHILDREN

CLOWNS

FLOWERS

GAMES

GARDEN

GAZEBO

GRASS

GRILL

HOPSCOTCH

ICE CREAM

JOGGERS

JUGGLERS

KITE

LANDSCAPE

LAWN

LEMONADE

PICNIC

PIGEONS

PLANTS

PLAYGROUND

POND

POOL

RECREATION

ROSES

SANDBOX

SHADE

SHELTER

SKATEBOARD

SLIDE

SWIMMING

SWINGS

TABLES

```
H C N E B L A N K E T I K J
M X B D P R E T L E H S Y M
Q O I G N I M M I W S E W Q
I B K E Q O G J O G G E R S
T D E O G H P E J N P Q H P
A N R N P M O U O L A A M L
B A S A O J G P A N D D A N
L S E C O G I Y S E S W E E
E S M U L B G S P C N V R R
S V R E C R E A T I O N C D
S G R E O E C T R N C T E L
A S N U W S B R A D A N C I
R Q N I D O K R O K E L I H
G D S N W O L C A S S N P C
D G A M E S Z F O B E Z A G
L L I R G A P E D I L S C B
```

Solution on Page 323

ANIMAL

BACK

BAGS

BLANKET

BOOTS

BROWN

BUCKLE

CAMEL

CANTLE

CHAPS

CINCH

COMFORT

COWBOY

CUSHION

ENGLISH

EQUINE

FENDERS

GIRTH

HARNESS

HORN

HUNTING

JOCKEY

LOAD

MOUNT

OIL

PAD

POMMEL

PONY

RANCH

REIN

RIDE

RODEO

SEAT

SHOES

SIT

SOAP

STABLE

STRAP

STYLE

TACK

```
B J C B S H C N A R I D E W
O D O O E D O R P T U K N J
X G A C M S W L N A A R C Y
M P N K K F B U C B R O W N
H T R I G E O F A O P T N O
O L O Y T M Y R N O B A S P
K L B L A N K E T T U E D G
Q D W O I O U Q L S C S Q V
K E N G L I S H E S K C A B
S C X O A H L L E E L Y T S
T E A Y M S R E D N E F S G
I D L T I U L M C R I P M C
S G A B N C A M I A A U D Z
Y O W Y A R E O N H M O Q K
V R S S D T O P C N I E R E
G S S E O H S H H H L Z Q L S
```

Solution on Page 324

ACRYLIC

ART

BLACK

CLASS

CLEAN

COLOR

COMPUTER

DIAGRAM

DRY

EDUCATION

ERASE

GLOSSY

IDEA

INK

LECTURE

LESSON

MAGNETS

MESSAGE

NOTES

OFFICE

OVERHEAD

PEN

PLASTIC

PRESENTATION

PROJECT

SCHOOL

SMOOTH

STEEL

STUDENT

SURFACE

TEACHER

VIRTUAL

WALL

WHITE

WORK

WRITE

```
Y N D K X K Z O C T L B F G
E L A U T R I V O W R D S S
T L S E T O N E M K P N T L
I O C K L W V R P N O E E B
R O J C Y C N H U I E C N M
W H L A M X S E T L T P G A
Y C I L Y R C A E U L L A W
C S T B X N T D R Y Q B M K
I M S N O N T E C A F R U S
T R E S E D U C A T I O N D
S V S S A D I T E A C H E R
A E E B S L U A Q J W I G E
L R I D E A C T G C O L O R
P Y S S O L G E S R A R T A
L R O F F I C E L T A E P S
X D E T I H W H T O O M S E
```

Solution on Page 324

ACADEMY

ARREST

ARSON

BADGE

BATON

BEAT

BURGLARY

BUST

CANINE

CAPTAIN

CHIEF

CITATION

DRAGNET

DUTY

FLARE

GUN

HOLSTER

HOMICIDE

JAIL

JUDGE

LAPD

MACE

MURDER

NYPD

ORDER

PAROLE

PARTNER

PRISON

PROTECT

RADIO

SAFETY

SIREN

STATION

SUSPECT

SWAT

TICKET

TRAFFIC

UNIFORM

VICTIM

WARRANT

```
B R B S U D B M C H I E F V
V S A E T B U I S W A T O N Q
I I D A A S T Q L R E D R U M
R R I T T C Y M P A R T N E R
E E O L I A J P C R C T D G O
N N R V O W R S E E Q I T D F
F I D N N I A T P A C C C A I
I G E M S F S S F I Y K A B N
G Z R O E L U E M L R E N A U
N N N T O S N O I T A T I C G
D D Y H T X H E C E L R N A V
V N C R S F L E C N G A E D M
Y Y O Q E O T A E G R F G E M
M P F S R O M O X A U F D M D
D D W A R R A N T R B I U Y J
R R P P A A L A P D J C J G X
```

Solution on Page 324

AUTOMATIC

BIND

BOOKLET

BULLETIN

BUSINESS

CLIP

CONNECT

DESK

DEVICE

DOCUMENT

ELECTRIC

FASTEN

FILES

GUN

HEAVY

JAMMED

JOIN

LARGE

LOAD

MANUAL

MECHANICAL

METAL

OFFICE

PAPER

PIN

PUNCH

PUSH

SCHOOL

SHEET

STAPLE

SUPPLIES

SURGICAL

TACK

TEACHER

TOGETHER

TOOL

WORK

Solution on Page

```
O P G G A Y S E I L P P U S
D Q M A U T O M A T I C M T
L E U M D N H C L I P A Y A
O V M B U S I N E S S V S P
A B E M X N M A N U A L A L
D U L L A T E M R E B P O E
O L E H A J Q G H S E U B C
C L C O F F I C E R V S I W
U E T T A C K L M Y K H N O
M T R O A E I T B N P S D R
E I I L G F C K O E U C E K
N N C R S E Y M O T N H V D
T Z A V N H T L K S C O I P
O L J N I P E H L A H O C X
O F O Q O U B E E F T L E Y
L C A V J J J J T T R Y N J G
```

Solution on Page 324

AUDIENCE

BETWEEN

BRIDE

BUS

CART

CENTER

CHAIRS

CHURCH

CLEAR

CONCERT

COURT

DOWN

FACTORY

FOOD

LANE

LIGHTS

LINE

LONG

MALL

MARKET

MIDDLE

MOVIE

NUMBER

PASSAGE

PATH

PEW

RETAIL

ROW

SEAT

SECTION

SHELVES

SHOP

SPACE

STADIUM

STORE

THEATER

USHER

WALK

WEDDING

WIDE

```
L P E N J C H G C N Z V I Z
A T O E I V O M R A S B M E
N P D H P R O W U H R I B L
E R O T S R P H E I D T W I
V P W L R A B L D D D I F G
A I N J S E V E L Z D A V H
U X W S T E C E S E C I T T
D C A W S L C N G T S A N S
I G E E O O R T O R P F W G
E E A N U E E R I C O M A M
N T G R T C Y A E O M A L L
C L T A A E H J D T N R K L
E S I P A C R U E E A K W O
B L S N U M B E R C L E A R
H M E D E P U Z W C P T H K
F X Z T O F S W U S H E R T
```

Solution on Page 325

AIR	MACHINE
BATTERY	MECHANIC
BELTS	MOTOR
BLOCK	OIL
BURN	PARTS
CAR	PISTON
CONVERT	POWER
COOLING	PROPEL
CYLINDER	REV
DIESEL	ROCKET
DRIVE	RUN
ELECTRIC	SPEED
EMISSION	STEAM
ENERGY	STIRLING
ENGINEER	TORQUE
EXHAUST	TURBINE
FUEL	VALVES
GAS	VEHICLE
GEARS	
HEAT	
HYDRAULIC	
JET	

```
F D T O K S M O T O R V S H
T E K C O R E E N I G N E A
O E L G R A L P J S Y A X R
R P E Y R E T T A B T R H S
Q S P R C G D I U S Q M A E
U N O T D K R N T R E B U V
E O R R L C A I I C B T S L
T I P A I O R M H L J I T A
C S H C I L U A R D Y H N V
O S H K I B N C J D D C N E
O I A N Z I R H D E S O E H
L M G G C E V I R D T N P I
I E W S W R E N L S E V A C
N U R O O S R E I R A E R L
G K P I E U U P G Y M R T E
W T H L B F I Y B E L T S R
```

Solution on Page 325

BAND	ORNAMENT
BOX	PEARL
BRIDE	PLATINUM
CEREMONY	PRECIOUS
CIRCLE	PRESENT
CLASS	PROMISE
COMMITMENT	ROUND
DESIGN	RUBY
DIAMOND	SAPPHIRE
EMERALD	SETTING
ENGRAVED	SILVER
EXPENSIVE	SIZE
FASHION	STERLING
GEM	STYLE
GIFT	TITANIUM
GOLD	TOE
GROOM	WEAR
HAND	WEDDING
JEWELS	
LOVE	
METAL	
OPAL	

```
R W Z P N G I S E D I R B C
W M E T A L G R O O M C J Y
V J U D M U I N A T I T B B
U E D R D H A N D O P U E U
Y W A N P I B E L C R I C T
Y E B P O R N A M E N T V N
W L A R K M E G P R Z H R E
O S N E S D A C G E M I V M
P C D S T E V I I M A I S T
A L F E E V Y S D O S R P I
L A A N R A E L T N U R L M
B S S T L R O V E Y O S F M
O S H G I G T P O M L L U O
X W I R N N X S I L V E R C
O F O X G E U S E T T I N G
T D N U O R E M E R A L D L
```

Solution on Page 325

ANNIVERSARY

APPETIZERS

BALLOONS

BEER

BIRTHDAY

BLOCK PARTY

CANDLES

CELEBRATION

CHRISTMAS

COCKTAIL

DECORATIONS

DRINKING

EATING

EVENT

FAMILY

FOOD

FUN

GAMES

GATHERING

GIFTS

GRADUATION

GROUP

GUESTS

HALLOWEEN

INVITATIONS

KEG

MIXER

MUSIC

PEOPLE

RECEPTION

STREAMERS

SURPRISE

TEA PARTY

TEENAGERS

```
R A P P E T I Z E R S A P R
Y G R A D U A T I O N E E G
B I R T H D A Y V N O X N F
E T N E V E R H I P I I U T
S E N Y I C B V L M T D F E
I A O L T O E E G A A R C E
R P I I G R E C E P T I O N
P A T M S A A S K R I N C A
R R A A F T T P T J V K K G
U T R F O I R H K F N I T E
S Y B Y O O Y E E C I N A R
T S E L D N A C A R O G I S
S C L C I S U M S M I L L E
E U E H A L L O W E E N B M
U T C H R I S T M A S R G A
G R O U P B A L L O O N S G
```

Solution on Page 325

ACRYLIC

AERIAL

BIND

BOAT

BRAID

BRIDGE

CABLE

CLIMB

CLOTH

COIL

CORD

COWBOY

CUT

FASTEN

FIBER

HEMP

JUMP

JUTE

KNOT

LENGTH

LINE

LONG

LOOP

MANILA

PLY

PULL

RANCH

RAYON

RODEO

SAFETY

SAIL

SHIP

SILK

SISAL

SWING

THICK

TIE

TOW

TUG

WHIP

```
D H W O M F J U T E G W H E
T L Y X T L L Y H N Q Y L P
A O P S A V F L I A S L I H
R J I W X I E W C P L O N G
R L H K B U S O K F U C E F
K I S E N M S I T N T L K M
P N R W M L I M S U B O L H
P O O L X P E L C A G T N H
E F O Y O B W O C B L H D K
T R R C A A L A I R E A R B
A O O H X R L W L I N D O A
C D W C L I O C Y D G A C Q
E E I N N L E E R G T T B X
R O S A F E T Y C E H I I M
M R M R R N O F A S T E N L
R I D M D B J U M P M E D U
```

Solution on Page 326

ADVENTURE

AIRSTREAM

AWNING

BED

CAR

COMFORT

COMPACT

DRIVING

FAMILY

FUN

GAS

HAUL

HIGHWAY

HITCH

HOME

HOUSE

JOURNEY

KITCHEN

LARGE

LEISURE

LIVE

LOAD

MOBILE

OUTDOORS

PARK

RIDE

ROAD

SEASONAL

SHELTER

SHOWER

SLEEP

SMALL

TIRES

TOW

TRAVEL

TRIP

TRUCK

VAN

VEHICLE

WHEEL

Solution on Page 000

```
V X A D V E N T U R E V I L
E S H I D S V N U F P M Y S
G L L A R G E V E H I C L E
T G I E U S Y A W H G I H R
Y Q P B E L T L S S C L E I
B H L S O P O R Y O X T D T
J T C A P M O C E P N F I Q
B C O M F O R T N A E A R K
I W O T D Q L V R R M M L C
T S H T C R E Y U K O I O U
H H U E X E I E O G H L A R
E O I C E T S V J N P Y D T
L W U T T L U L I I L G V D
D E B S C E R Z R N P R A C
H R F B E H E T Z W G O N S
E L L A M S L E V A R T D X
```

Solution on Page 326

ALMANAC

APPENDIX

AUTHOR

BOOKENDS

BUSINESS

CASE

CHAPTERS

CONCEPT

COOKING

COPYRIGHT

DRAMA

EDITION

FICTIONAL

FONT

FOOTNOTES

HARDCOVER

INDEX

ISBN

ISSUE

JACKET

LIBRARY

NOVELS

PAGES

PAPERBACK

PREFACE

PRINTING

PUZZLES

REFERENCE

REVIEW

ROMANCE

SERIES

SETTING

SHELF

STORY

TEXTBOOK

TUTORIAL

USED

```
A L M A N A C W E I V E R D
S I T F L E H S E R I E S R
E S E J O C A S E R K B S A
G B K C X O P H E P Y O P M
A N C O I P T F M R V O R A
P G A O D Y E N O I P K E U
U N J K N R R T O N A E F T
Z I E I E I S Y F T P N A H
Z T G N P G N I U I E D C O
L T C G P H C D S N R S E R
E E P B A T T W E G B L D O
S S E N I S U B D X A E I M
R E V O C D R A H C C V T A
F O N T E X T B O O K O I N
L A I R O T U T P E C N O C
L I B R A R Y E U S S I N E
```

Solution on Page 326

AGRICULTURE

BAKED GOODS

BALLOONS

BLUE RIBBON

BUMPER CARS

CARNIVAL

CAROUSEL

CLOWNS

COIN TOSS

COMPETITIONS

CONCESSIONS

CONTEST

COTTON CANDY

DANCERS

EXHIBITS

FOOD

FUN

GAMES

HANDICRAFTS

ICE CREAM

LIGHTS

LIVESTOCK

MUSIC

NOVELTIES

PICTURES

PIZZA

PRIZES

RACES

RIDE PASS

SNOW CONES

SWINGS

```
K S K E X H I B I T S Y B G
C O N C E S S I O N S G U A
O S S O T N I O C I S U M M
T S M S N O W C O N E S P E
S A A G R I C U L T U R E S
E P E N J T F U N H S Y R N
V E R I G I I O U A D T C O
I D C W B T V A C N O P A O
L I E S R E C N A D O I R L
I R C I L P V C R I G C S L
G W I T R M N D N C D T C A
H I I I N O B B I R E U L B
T E Z G T C H E V A K R O D
S E J T P I Z Z A F A E W O
S C O N T E S T L T B S N O
G C S E C A R O U S E L S F
```

Solution on Page 326

ALPHABET

ANTIQUE

BACKSPACE

BROTHER

BUSINESS

CAPS LOCK

CARRIAGE

CARTRIDGE

DESK

DICTATION

DING

FINGERS

FONT

IBM

INVENTION

KEYBOARD

LETTERS

MACHINE

MANUAL

NOISY

NUMBERS

OFFICES

OLIVETTI

PORTABLE

PRINT

QWERTY

REMINGTON

RETURN

ROLLER

ROYAL

SCHOOL

SECRETARY

SELECTRIC

SPEED

STRIKE

TAPE

TYPIST

WPM

WRITING

```
L A Y O R E L L O R M P W Y
L A U N A M F P R I N T S Z
E D H N O I T N E V N I K C
T I K E N I H C A M O B S I
T N S G B N O T G N I M E R
E G E A L P H A B E T B C T
R R D I K C O L S P A C R C
S R A R J X A S D C T Y E E
R E N R U T E R K I C K T L
E H T A M N A S T Q I W A E
B T I C I O P T W R D Q R S
M O Q S B A E E T S I P Y T
U R U Y C V R S P E E D C A
N B E E I T W R I T I N G P
S K P L Y K P O R T A B L E
T N O F F I C E S C H O O L
```

Solution on Page 327

BATH

BRAID

BRIDLE

BRISTLE

BRUSH

BUCKET

CARE

CLEAN

CLIP

COAT

COMB

CURRY

DIRT

GROOM

HAIR

HAND

HARNESS

HEALTH

HOOF

HORSE

MANE

MUD

PICK

POLISH

SADDLE

SCRAPER

SHINE

SHOW

SKIN

SPONGE

SPRAY

STALL

TACK

TAIL

TEETH

THRUSH

TRIM

WASH

WATER

WET

Horse Grooming

```
C T H W H C O E O Y B Q P A
T G E E G N O P S R N O S H
H E S W A T E R I R L O T N
R A P J C L T S D I R T A G
U E R O O E T O S A D D L E
S H A N K L L H O R S E L N
H T Y C E X F D I T U S L A
R M U B C S K I N Q P L S M
P B O M Q H S U R B E N M R
D R T O I C L E A N A T W D
U I C C R C C L I P S T O Y
M D A A U G X H T E E T H C
M L P R R S S O A A W A S H
I E R I B E E O P N I J H C
R Y A K C A T F W T D L V M
T H O X D K M Z Z X F I D W
```

Solution on Page 327

BIG	LUNCH
BUFFET	MENU
CANTEEN	MILK
CASHIER	OFFICE
CHAIR	PIZZA
COFFEE	PLAN
COLLEGE	QUICK
COOK	REGISTER
COUNTER	ROOM
CUPS	SALAD
DINE	SERVER
DISHES	SNACKS
DRINK	STALL
EAT	STORE
FACILITY	STUDENT
FOOD	TABLE
HALL	TRAY
HOT	VARIETY
HUNGRY	
KITCHEN	
LINE	
LOUD	

```
Y O E H W C H B F L F E O T
K T N R R E I H S A C Z V J
W Y I K E G E L L O C E L H
C N D L G T E F F U B C S O
O A Z Z I P N E H C T I K V
V L N E S C M U F O V F C G
E P V T T E A Q O F T F A T
A P C A E N H F O C O O N Q
T M O O R E E S D T O C S B
R L I Z T I N D I D A O A W
A I S E R V E R U D S B K N
Y S A L A D E T B T R P L P
H T T H U N G R Y L S I U E
B A W K C I U Q O A I N N C
U L L I N E D U Z T E V C K
Q L K L I M D O Z M S V H M
```

Solution on Page 327

AIRCRAFT	PING
AIRPORT	PLANES
ALTITUDE	POLICE
ANTENNA	PULSE
ARMY	RAIN
AVIATION	RANGE
BATS	SCAN
BEARING	SCREEN
BLIP	SHIP
DETECT	SIGNAL
DISH	SONAR
DOPPLER	SOUND
ECHO	SPY
ENERGY	STEALTH
FORECAST	STORM
JAMMING	SYSTEM
LOCATION	WAR
MEASURE	WEATHER
MILITARY	
MISSILE	
NAVY	
OBJECT	

```
A X V U H H Z M L H W A R R
R R A N G E N E R G Y V A N S
M I P A S I G N A L I V A T
Y U M I S S I L E N N L H O
P R F O N M B A T S O N A R
S E U T M G W P O L I C E M
P N S A S E L O C A T I O N
D H J L A A M S T E A L T H
N T S T U D C I B L I P C B
E C H I Z P N E L T V W E C
E E I T F A R C R I A P J M
R T P U E C H O N O T L B E
C E P D O P P L E R F A O T
S D I E E R U S A E M N R S
T S G N I R A E B T F E C Y
H W M A N T E N N A C S G S
```

Solution on Page 327

ACTIVE

ATHLETIC

BEEFY

BIG

BRAWNY

BRUISING

BULKY

CAPABLE

DURABLE

ENDURING

ENERGETIC

FIRM

FORCEFUL

FORCIBLE

HEALTHY

HEFTY

HULKING

HUNK

HUSKY

MIGHTY

MUSCULAR

POTENT

POWERFUL

ROBUST

RUGGED

SECURE

SINEWY

SOLID

SOUND

STABLE

STALWART

STAUNCH

STEADY

STOUT

STURDY

TIRELESS

UNTIRING

VIGOROUS

VITAL

Powerful Words

```
B H H U S K Y S O U N D L L
E U U S E C U R E L B A T S
E N L N S E Y T N E T O P W
F K K K H E A L T H Y O V O
Y D I F Y K L B R A W N Y L
W U N O S N S E D E G G U R
E R G R U N T I R I N G G O
N A N C O R O F D I L O S B
I B I E R A U H E F T Y A U
S L R F O L T R A W L A T S
T E U U G U Y D R U T S H T
E V D L I C F O R C I B L E
A I N A V S C A P A B L E G
D T E T G U I H C N U A T S
Y C F I R M I N Y T H G I M
N A B V E N E R G E T I C D
```

Solution on Page 328

ARTIFICIAL

BASIN

BOAT

CITY

CLEAN

CONCRETE

CONSTRUCT

CONTROL

CREATED

DAM

DEEP

DIVER

DRINK

DROUGHT

FILL

FISH

FLOW

GROUND

LAKE

LEVEL

MAINTAIN

NATURAL

OIL

POTABLE

POWER

PUMPING

RAIN

RIVER

SERVICE

SOURCE

SPILLWAY

STORE

STREAM

SUPPLY

SWIMMING

TOWER

TURBINES

VALLEY

WATER

WELL

```
E G S R I V E R E W O P D I
B L E V E L L S S O U R C E
W P B A S I N I C M I R N D
N O V A L L E Y P N E I R I
T A L L T X J I K A A O T V
H S I F C O N S T R U C T E
D F S S F G P E T G O S Y R
S N P W Y T D I H N I E Y E
Z A I I T B F T C I L R L W
I T L M I I O R M A O V P O
P U L M C L E A N T R I P T
W R W I R T D B T N T C U D
A A A N E T U R B I N E S E
T L Y G R O U N D A O K G E
E R O T S T R E A M C A I P
R T K P P S S W W E L L Q O
```

Solution on Page 328

BILLS

BLACK

BREAST

BROWN

BUSINESS

CARD

CASE

CHAIN

CLASP

CLIP

COINS

CREDIT

CURRENCY

DESIGNER

FABRIC

FASHION

FLAT

FOLD

HANDBAG

HOLDER

JEANS

LEATHER

LICENSE

LOST

MEN

MONEY

NOTES

NYLON

PANTS

PERSONAL

PHOTO

PLASTIC

POCKET

PURSE

SLOTS

SMALL

STOLEN

STORAGE

TRAVEL

VELCRO

```
O M U W L L A M S F O L D S
T N E M O B Y T U T O U R T
O O A S R E H F Y B O C I U
H L T O N E L O T S L L I B
P Y W O H A N D B A G A S P
C N M E T O Y G E B E S C T
I C H A I N D W I S S P I K
R E V H R T B W R S S D U L
B G S C E R C U R R E N C Y
A A A K E O P L J R N D I L
F R C A I J S E C F I T R O
D O S Z C E L A N O S R E P
P T N P L A S T I C U A D A
I S I P N N S H Q X B V L N
L N O T E S N E C I L E O T
C Z C V E L C R O T C L H S
```

Solution on Page 328

ADDITIVE

ALMOND

AROMA

BANANA

BITTER

BLAND

CHERRY

COOK

EAT

ENHANCE

FOOD

FRUIT

GARLIC

GOOD

GRAPE

HOT

LEMON

MINT

MOUTH

NATURAL

ODOR

ORANGE

PEPPER

RICH

SALT

SAVOR

SCENT

SENSE

SHARP

SMELL

SOUR

SPICE

SUGAR

SWEET

TANG

TART

TASTE

VANILLA

VINEGAR

WINE

```
O T A N G X H H C I R I H C
C D D O P L B O S O U R A D
A C O D W B L H T U O M E A
D D O R A I A E Y S O K C R
N Y F E B S N N M R E I I M
H H R V I T D E A S C N P T
Y Z U R E M I N T N E C S E
T G I A E A L L I N A V H E
A A T E N H A N C E I C A W
B R R P Y R C F V N E A R S
R L X T U L V I E G S U P T
B I T T E R T G N V R A A A
E C A M A I A A D Q G A L S
P N O G D R R E P P E P P T
Q N U D N O M L A G N F D E
L S A V O R O X G G V F F C
```

Solution on Page 328

ANIMATION

BATTERY

BLINKING

BRIGHT

BULB

CIRCUIT

COLOR

COMPUTER

CORD

DISPLAY

ENERGY

FIBER

FLASHING

FLICKER

FUSE

GLASS

HOLIDAY

HOUSE

LAMPS

LED

LIGHT

ORNAMENT

OUTSIDE

PLASTIC

PLUG

POWER

SAFETY

SETS

SHOW

SIGN

SOCKET

STAR

STRAND

STRING

SWITCH

TIMER

TREE

VOLTAGE

WATTS

WIRES

Christmas Display

```
S T T A W P O W E R E B I F
S W I T C H L L S Y N Y B R
A O S T J C R U T T E G A A
L A C P R E O E G H R B I T
G N C K M E F R B O G A O S
X I S I E A E B D L Y I N T
K M T L S T L G J I U H R D
S A E X U I N T W D W B S B
G T S P N I I E I A O A E I
C I M K R U S O M Y H T R L
Q O I T C U U P L A S T I C
C N S R O T H G I L N E W O
G N I H S A L F C P G R Z L
Y C L I U N R F U S E Y O O
L E D Y N R E K C I L F L R
H E G A T L O V U D C T R F
```

Solution on Page 329

ABSINTHE

BEER

BOOZE

CHAMPAGNE

CIDER

COCKTAIL

COFFEE

COGNAC

COLA

EGGNOG

ESPRESSO

GINGER ALE

GRAPPA

GROG

HOOCH

LEMONADE

LIMEADE

LIQUEUR

MILK

MOONSHINE

NECTAR

ORANGEADE

OUZO

PASTIS

PULQUE

PUNCH

RAKI

RUM

RYE

SCOTCH

SLIVOVITZ

SPARKLING

SPIRITS

TEA

TOMATO JUICE

VODKA

WHISKEY

WINE

```
P Z V O D K A B B O O Z E D
T S I E S P R E S S O U O A
Y E P N K H C N U P Q X Z P
C E G I N G E R A L E V U P
Y F K H R Y F S U C W L O A
R F H S R I T P I H I E S R
S O C N I I T U S A J M C G
L C O O S H J S T M S O O R
I I O O R O W K E P J N T O
V D H M T A C C A A G A C G
O E R A U O N R A G E D H N
V R M C C R K G E N C E H E
I O O N K L I M E E G O V C
T A B S I N T H E A B O L T
Z W I N E L I M E A D E C A
S E G R A K I L I Q U E U R
```

Solution on Page 329

AMP	MAGNETIC
APPLIANCE	METER
ARC	MOTOR
BATTERY	OUTAGE
BULB	OUTLET
CIRCUIT	PLUG
COMPUTER	POTENTIAL
CONDUCTION	POWER
CORD	RESISTOR
COULOMB	SHOCK
CURRENT	SOURCE
EDISON	STATIC
ELECTRONS	SURGE
ENERGY	SWITCH
ENGINE	UTILITY
FIELD	VOLT
FORCE	WATTAGE
HEAT	WIRE
HOUSE	
INDUSTRY	
LIGHT	
LINES	

Electric

```
R D S S T A T I C L I N E S
H B U L B H I E T L O V N H
M O T O R M G N L Y O K I O
H G U L P A O I D T P S G C
E U R S C G O L L U U P N K
A Y G R E N E J U R S O E N
T B A T T E R Y G O I T R M
U T I L I T Y E S T C E R R
X A P P L I A N C E T N O Y
T F M K K C O U T U W T A H
N I D P U R D N P I S I O C
O E U R T N E M R I M A U T
S L P C O R O E S M E L T I
I D E C R C P E G A T T A W
D L I U H I R P O W E R G S
E E C R O F C S O U R C E S
```

Solution on Page 329

Electric

PUZZLES • 137

ANATOMY	MOVEMENT
ANIMAL	NECK
ARM	PATELLA
BLOOD	PELVIC
BODY	POROUS
BROKEN	RADIUS
CALCIUM	RIB
CAST	SCAPULA
DENSITY	SHAPE
FEMUR	SHOULDER
FIBULA	SKULL
FRAME	SPINE
HAND	STERNUM
HIP	STRONG
HUMAN	SUPPORT
INTERNAL	TENDONS
JAW	TIBIA
JOINT	ULNA
KNEE	
LEG	
LONG	
MINERAL	

Bone

```
C V S L E Z O O E G K L V S
V V P A P I A Q H U M A N U
X U I R A T N E M E V O M I
K Y N E H F A T D H D V C D
X D E N S I T Y E N G F S A
W O K I T B O Y E R J N H R
G B O M E U M T U L N A O Q
E M R R R L Y U A C H A U L
L J B A N A F Z I D O O L B
L O A P U E T S A C S A D N
U I R W M S C A P U L A E E
K N K U U D K E P L A A R C
S T R O N G L P E H M P C K
K I R A R V O T I B I A U L
B O H S I R A P X K N E E S
P O D C T P T F E M A R F P
```

Solution on Page 329

ADVICE	HUNGRY
BEDTIME	INFANT
BIRTH	JOY
BLANKET	LAMAZE
BOY	LITTLE
BUNDLE	MAMA
BURP	MOMMY
CHILD	MOTHER
COO	NURSE
CRY	POWDER
CUTE	RATTLE
DADDY	SAFETY
DAY CARE	SLEEP
DIAPERS	STINKY
FATHER	STORY
FEED	TOYS
FUN	TWINS
GIGGLE	WET
GIRL	
GRIN	
HAPPY	
HOME	

Baby Words

```
X D F U Z B O D O V J I K V
M C H G B S E O B C H I L D
O K I F S E T U C Y O A S A
F R T D F T N O M D M Y S D
L E M I T D E B R A E M Y D
K D O F L D C K Z Y M O O Y
U W T E W B I E N C J A T M
P O H I E U V A S A F E T Y
J P E S F R D H P R L E W O
R S R Y P P A H S E W B I B
G U E E X F A T H E R V N K
N B E L N L I T T L E S S U
Z L I O T N F Y R G N U H Z
S I H R K T A U B G Q C O H
A U J Y T N A F N I R G N E
F A F X H H Y R C G Y S H H
```

Solution on Page 330

ADVISORS

AMEX

ASSET

AVERAGES

BANKING

BROKER

CALL

CASH

CLOSE

COMPOUND

CRASH

DEBT

EARNINGS

ECONOMY

EQUITY

EXERCISE

FLOOR

FUTURES

HEDGING

INVESTOR

IRA

ISSUE

LOAD

MARGIN

MARKETS

MATURE

MONEY

NASDAQ

NYSE

OPTIONS

PLUMMET

PROXY

PUT

QUOTES

RALLY

TAXES

TICKER

TRADERS

VALUE

VOLUME

Investment Jargon

```
V A L U E I B R O K E R Z S
I E F D A O L P V C E Q D E
Y T I U Q E T O D A R U R X
D I X S T I L N V S U O U A
E C P E O U U E T H T T H T
B K G N M O R E C S A E F I
T E S E P A K E E O M S T R
R R R R M G R I V S Y N R E A
A N O E A R N I N G S O M L
D C S M Z I Y H Y N H O M L
E S I C R E X E S I E L U Y
R A V L R C O D E K A F L L
S P D O M A R G I N S K P H
C R A S H L P I N A S D A Q
M O N E Y L G N Z B E X X R
W R I S S U E G Z R T U P I
```

Solution on Page 330

ANTS	FLAME
BASTING	FOIL
BBQ	FRUIT
BEER	GAMES
BLANKET	GRASS
BRAZIER	GRILL
BREAD	KIDS
BUNS	MEAT
CAKE	OLIVES
CATCH	PARK
CHEESE	PEPPER
CHICKEN	PIT
COKES	RADIO
COLAS	ROAST
COOLER	SALT
CORN	SAUCE
CUPS	STEAKS
DATE	TONGS
EGGS	
EMBERS	
FAMILY	
FIRE	

Solution on Page

```
C A E R I F K I D S C Q J N
B P M A E P Y M R H A B W X
C M S B L E T R E R T L A Y
X C S S P P B E L K C E O R
K K P S M P S I O F H C C C
I W G E A E Z Z O E O H J I
U G A M S R V A C G R I L L
E T F A S G G R S P U C L W
Y J U L K A E B A S E K O C
I C P F A M I L Y D T E K N
E I Y R E E B A S T I N G T
T D Y U T S R N E R P O A N
A M U I S N E K V S E A B N
D Q A T A U A E I A P B R P
Y X W C O B D T L L Q O M K
Y H Q R R S G N O T C A K E
```

Solution on Page 330

ARTISTS

BALLADS

BAND

BASS GUITAR

CHANTS

CHICAGO

CONCERT

COUNTRY

DRUMS

HARMONICA

HYMNS

INSTRUMENTS

JAZZ

LEAD BELLY

MAJOR SCALE

MELANCHOLY

MEMPHIS

MOOD

MUSIC GENRE

MUSICIANS

NEW ORLEANS

NOTES

PITCH

PLAY

RECORDS

ROCK

SADNESS

SAXOPHONE

SHOUTS

SINGERS

SINGING

SLOW

SPIRITUALS

TROMBONE

VOCALS

WORK SONGS

```
P S L A U T I R I P S L O W
M L I E Y H R E C O R D S Y
E A A N A R A E S N M Y H E
M C P Y G D T R C Z Z A J N
P O C I L I B N M N G D S O
H V S W T O N E U O O U N H
I N T K O C H G L O N C A P
S E N E C R H C M L C I I O
D W E S N O K I N Y Y O C X
A O M A J O R S C A L E I A
L R U D N A B U O A L I S S
L L R N D R U M S N G E U H
A E T E N S E T O N G O M O
B A S S G U I T A R Y S D U
V N N S H A R T I S T S P T
E S I N G E R S T N A H C S
```

Solution on Page 330

ACADEMIA

APPLE

ARITHMETIC

ASSIGNMENT

ATTENDANCE

BLACKBOARD

BOOK

BUS

CAMPUS

CLASS

COLLEGE

COURSE

CURRICULUM

DESK

EDUCATION

ENGLISH

EXAM

GPA

GYM

HOMEWORK

LESSON

LITERATURE

LOUNGE

MATH

PAPER

PENCIL

PRINCIPAL

PUPIL

QUIZ

READING

RECESS

RED PEN

SCHOLAR

STUDY

SUBJECT

TEACHER

TEST

TEXT

VARSITY

WRITING

```
T Y E X A M R M L I C N E P
E K F W I R E Y D U T S H R
A R X R M P A G S X R S V S
C O U I E A D L E U I G S U
H W M T D P I T O L P A B B
E E U I A E N C G H L M L J
R M L N C R G N A C C O A E
G O U G A L E S S O N S C C
P H C Q U I Z T S O D P K T
A C I T E M H T I R A M B E
V A R S I T Y T G L T A O G
P P R E C N A D N E T T A N
U P U T I C E G M C J H R U
P L C U U S S S E C E R D O
I E T D K P R I N C I P A L
L R E D P E N U T K O O B R
```

ART

BLACK

BOOK

COLOR

COMPUTER

COPY

DESIGN

DIGITAL

DOT MATRIX

FAX

FONT

GUTENBERG

IMAGE

INK

LASER

LETTERS

LITHOGRAPHY

MEDIA

MIMEOGRAPH

NEWS

OFFSET

PAGES

PAMPHLET

PEN

PICTURES

PLATES

POSTER

PRESS

PROCESS

PRODUCTION

PUBLISH

ROLLER

SCREEN

STAMP

TECHNOLOGY

TEXT

TONER

TRANSFER

WOODBLOCK

WORDS

Printing

```
S C R E E N E F X W Z T K S
P R O D U C T I O N J C R F
U H L S S E R P B N O E P A
B P L R E T S O P L T J L X
L A E D A C O G B T E L A L
I R R M I K O D E W L K T I
S G T E Y G O L O N H C E T
H O R S N O I R O L P A S H
D E A E W O D T A R M L S O
T M N R B S T S A G A B S G
X I S U A N E K L L P U E R
E M F T X R E T U P M O C A
T E E C O P Y T E S F F O P
N D R I M A G E U S W K R H
E I E P K D E S I G N E P Y
P A G E S T A M P I M L N V
```

AEROSPACE	PAINT
AIRCRAFT	PIPE
ALLOY	PLATE
BICYCLE	PROPERTIES
BUILDING	RARE
CHEMICAL	RESISTANT
COMPOUNDS	ROCKS
DENSE	RODS
DIOXIDE	RUTILE
DURABLE	SOLID
ELEMENT	STRENGTH
ENGINES	STRONG
EXPENSIVE	STURDY
HARD	SUBMARINES
ILMENITE	SURGICAL
INDUSTRIAL	TITANS
JEWELRY	TOUGH
LIGHT	WATCH
MEDICAL	
METAL	
MINE	
ORE	

Solution on Page

```
H G U O T J E W E L R Y E P
W D I L O S S N A T I T I Q
S E I C N D G Z M P A P K R
U X N E O I R E R L E A L L
B P D R N M T O P D I R I A
M E U E C A P S O R E A G C
A N S R L E R O C K S R H I
R S T U R D Y R U T T E T G
I I R T X I A E C N M S S R
N V I I A F L M E I D I T U
E E A L T C E M C A R S R S
S K L E Y D E A E P A T O H
F O N C I L L V W N H A N C
Y I I C E B U I L D I N G T
M B A F T S T R E N G T H A
E L B A R U D I O X I D E W
```

Solution on Page 331

ACCELERATOR

AIR FILTER

ANTENNA

ASHTRAY

BATTERY

BUCKET SEAT

CAMSHAFT

CHASSIS

CHOKE

CLUTCH

COMBUSTION

CRANKCASE

CYLINDER

DASHBOARD

DEFROSTER

EXHAUST

FENDER

FUSE

GAS GAUGE

HEADREST

HOOD

HORN

IGNITION

ODOMETER

OIL

RADIATOR

SEAT BELT

SPEEDOMETER

STEERING

TAILLIGHT

TANK

THROTTLE

TIRE

WINDSHIELD

Solution on P

```
A P J Z T A I L L I G H T F
E X H A U S T H R O T T L E
T I R E T E M O D O O H E N
W P N O I T S U B M O C B D
I K N A T H E A D R E S T E
N G A S G A U G E T R S A R
D B A T T E R Y A O N I E E
S P E E D O M E T E R S S T
H Y A R T H S A L G O S A S
I I G N I T I O N E H A C O
E H A R E D N I L Y C H K R
L C U K A I R E K O H C N F
D T C R R E T L I F R I A E
F U S E E D A S H B O A R D
B L Y T N T F A H S M A C W
H C S L I O A N N E T N A K
```

Solution on Page 331

ASH

BOILER

BRICK

BUILDING

BURNING

CAP

CLEAN

COMBUSTION

CONCRETE

COWL

CREOSOTE

DAMPER

DIRTY

DRAFT

FIRE

FLUE

FUMES

FUNNEL

FURNACE

HEAT

HIGH

HOT

LINER

LOGS

MANTLE

MORTAR

OUTSIDE

ROCK

ROOF

SANTA

SMOKE

SOOT

STACK

STONE

STRUCTURE

SWEEP

TALL

VENT

WARMTH

WOOD

```
R C E E U L F E Q G Y B L E
V P O D O O W R R N R E A Q
R K I B E N F O Y I N L S W
K W M D U U E C C N F T G K
B T Q E R I W K U R R Y O L
O Q Y N T A L F Q U Q S L N
I N A F R O F D C B M O K N
L C O M B U S T I O N O C R
E O T A E H U O K N X T A S
R H A S T R M E E H G C T W
R G T R E P M A D R L S S E
L I N E R N D P N E C T E E
L H A N C T I R A T R O M P
A V S E N T R N S C L N U X
T D H E O U T S I D E E F D
W G V H C B Y Z Y V O Z J K
```

Solution on Page 332

ALARM

ALERT

BEACON

BOATS

CAPTAIN

CIRCULAR

CLIFF

CRASH

CREW

DANGER

DARKNESS

DISTANCE

FOG

GUIDE

HARBOR

HAZARD

HORIZON

KEEPER

LAMPS

LENS

MAINE

MIRRORS

NIGHT

OCEAN

ROCKS

ROTATE

SAFETY

SAILORS

SCANNING

SEASIDE

SHOALS

SIGNAL

SKY

STORMS

TALL

TOURISTS

TOWERS

WARNING

WATCHMAN

WAVES

```
I W L V T W E R C R A S H L
A L A R M D W L J S E V A W
B L E T G W I Y T E F A S K
O L H S C F I S R O R R I M
A A O A F H I S T O R M S Y
T T E I R R M S E A S I D E
S D T L U B D A R K N E S S
E R A O R X O A N R O C K S
N A T R I E L R N O C A E B
I Z O S Y U G U I D E S E T
A A R S C A N N I N G L P O
M H O R I Z O N A D O A E W
G N I N R A W Z D D F O R E
O C A P T A I N N I G H T R
Y K S P M A L A N G I S O S
O C E A N L E N S E Y Y N H
```

Solution on Page 332

ACRYLIC

ART

BED

BITE

BODY

BREAK

BRITTLE

BROKEN

BUFF

CHIP

CLAW

CLEAN

CLIP

CUT

DERMIS

DIGIT

DIRTY

FAKE

FEET

FILE

FINGER

FOOT

FUNGUS

GROW

HAND

KERATIN

LONG

LUNULA

MAMMALS

PAINT

PLATE

POLISH

RIDGES

ROOT

TAP

THUMB

TIPS

TOE

TRIM

WHITE

Nails

```
A V O R Z M B B B Q E L I F Y
P C U T M E S A T O O F A P
D C R H D L R E G N I F K Q
S H R Y A T P A I N T U E A
F I Z M L T X T C E A B T N
R P M J B I A F F X X E A C
J A I R R R C P L U N U L A
M T R T E B R O K E N A P C
C O T K A D T L Q Y W G O N
H E S I K R E I H T L G U T
J P P H T P T S G R H O R S
Z O J O E T I H W I Y A N E
K O O Z E I B L U D D W N G
B R L H F P N S C M O L J D
C M V F K S H S M R B L D I
O J W N M T W S G D G B Q R
```

Solution on Page 332

PUZZLES • 161

BAKED ALASKA

BANANA SPLIT

BOWL

CAKE

CARAMEL

CHERRIES

CHURN

COLD

CONES

CREAMY

CUP

DAIRY QUEEN

DISH

FAT

FLAVORS

FREEZER

FRUIT

FUDGE

GELATO

LICK

MILK

NEAPOLITAN

NUTS

PARLOR

PIE

SANDWICH

SCOOP

SHERBET

SMOOTH

SNACK

SORBET

SPOON

STRAWBERRY

SUMMER

SWEET

SYRUP

TREAT

TUB

VANILLA

VENDOR

```
P O O C S X B C E K A C T C
V A N I L L A Y P X O R E O
S B R W A R K R U T S E B L
U O O L A R E R R O A A R D
M B R M O T D E Y T N M E Q
M E E B F R A B S A D Y H S
E L Z L E T L W N L W B S P
R B E K I T A A A E I U S O
G S E N O C S R C G C T P O
R M R U U P K T K C H U R N
O F F P L G A S R O V A L F
D D A I R Y Q U E E N T G R
N A T I L O P A E N J E X U
E G D U F C H E R R I E S I
V M I L K H T O O M S W I T
G R B N U T S U K D I S H P
```

Solution on Page 332

AUTHORITY

BATTLE

BOSTON

BUNKER HILL

COLONISTS

CONCORD

CONSTITUTION

COURAGE

DECLARATION

DEMOCRACY

ENGLAND

FLAG

GOVERNANCE

INDEPENDENCE

JEFFERSON

JOHN ADAMS

KING GEORGE

LEXINGTON

LIBERTY

LOYALISTS

NATION

PATRIOTS

POLITICS

SOVEREIGNTY

STAMP ACT

TAXATION

TEA PARTY

```
T C A P M A T S Y E I O S S
E G A R U O C C G T Y C T O
A S D E C L A R A T I O N S
P O M Q F R O X R T I O M C
A V M V C E A E I R I A O F
R E O O G T B L T T D N K Q
T R M G I I O A U A C Y C L
Y E N O L P P T N O T S O B
D I N V L L I H R E K N U B
K G A E H T O D N A L G N E
E N T R S J E F F E R S O N
L T I N D E P E N D E N C E
T Y O A U T H O R I T Y R F
T C N N L O Y A L I S T S L
A J A C O L O N I S T S Y A
B X L E X I N G T O N S B G
```

Solution on Page 333

ABILENE
BACON
BANK
BEANS
BEDROLL
BISCUIT
BOOTS
BRAWL
BRONCO
BUNK
CANYON
CATTLE
CORRAL
COWBOY
COYOTE
DEPUTY
DESERT
DRIVE
DUEL
DUSTY
FENCES
FORTS

GULCH
HERO
HIDE
HORSES
JAIL
JEANS
JERKY
LAND
LARIAT
LASSO
REINS
RIFLE
ROAM
RODEO
ROPE
SADDLE
SPURS
WATER

```
E U W L R E T A W O D E Z K
M V G A I A H I D E E L O E
Y R I R I S N A E B P F X T
L L O R D E B I S C U I T Y
W P A O D I R G E A T R O R
E L D C L H O B R N Y B S Z
S N A E J E N I T Y W Q S U
B U N K T R C L E O L I A J
K E O Y R O O T C N H G L H
S L C U K E Y S T R O F B C
H T A D D R I O S B R A W L
B T B O U F E N C E S O Y U
G A R O L J C J S T E T A G
A C N A O E L D D A S A T M
Z Y N K F T U S R U P S A J
G D U H P U S D D O M G D X
```

Solution on Page 333

ADAMS

ANDERSON

BAKER

BROWN

CAMPBELL

CARTER

CLARK

DAVIS

GARCIA

GREEN

HALL

HARRIS

HERNANDEZ

HILL

JACKSON

JOHNSON

JONES

KING

LEE

LOPEZ

MARTIN

MITCHELL

MOORE

NELSON

PARKER

PEREZ

ROBERTS

ROBINSON

RODRIGUEZ

SCOTT

SMITH

TAYLOR

THOMAS

TURNER

WALKER

WHITE

WILLIAMS

WILSON

WRIGHT

YOUNG

Common Family Names

```
L L A H H T I M S M G L S Q
T C N A S M A D A E A T E R
G H A R B R O W N Z R X O E
N N G R T U S C X E C B T K
O A O I T A J I B D I M J L
S P N S R E N O V N A O R A
K A M E L W R D S A H O O W
C Q M O E E L O E N D R L G
A A P O K R N L S R U E Y N
J E M R H G G O I E S W A U
Z C A P N T N G S H N O T O
K P X I B P U W I L S O N Y
B A K E R E N R U T V Q J Z
P E R E Z L L E H C T I M O
H G S M A I L L I W H I T E
T T O C S A A P K R A L C F
```

Solution on Page 333

PUZZLES • **169**

ADDITION

ANALYSIS

BUDGET

CALC

CELL

CHART

COLUMN

DATA

DYNAMIC

ENTRY

EXPORT

FILE

FINANCE

FONT

FOOTERS

GRAPH

GRID

HEADERS

IMPORT

INSERT

LINES

LIST

LOTUS

MATH

MODEL

NUMBER

OFFICE

PAPER

RANGE

RECORDS

REPORT

ROW

SHEET

SUM

TABLE

TEXT

TOOL

TOTAL

VALUE

WORK

```
Q D L I S T E X T R S I D F
T I A D D I T I O N E S R T
E R Y Y Q Y S W R C N U J P
B G E Q R U N Y N F I L E F
T M U S T T P A L T L V C K
L J S O N N N T M A A E E H
A K L E S I U E O I N B L H
L H B H F W F M T T C A L Y
D O E X P O R T B R A N G E
A E O I N N O T S E O L W R
T U I T B M M T R C R P Z E
A L H F N U O M E O L N M C
P A P E R L D V D R P A E I
E V A C P O E G A D S E C F
Q T R A H C L F E S W B R F
X R G W O R K S H T A M P O
```

Solution on Page 333

ABSTRACT

AIRPORT

ATLAS

CAPITALS

CELESTIAL

CITY

COMPASS

COUNTY

DEGREES

DESIGN

DIRT

DISTANCE

DIVIDED

EAST

EQUATOR

GLOBES

GRID

HIGHWAY

HOSPITAL

KEY

LEGEND

MAPS

MILES

MOUNTAIN

NAUTICAL

PARK

PAVED

RAILROAD

RELIEF

RIVER

SCALE

SCHOOL

SHADED

SOUTH

STREET

SYMBOLS

TITLE

TOWN

TRAVEL

WEST

```
T O W N Y E K R A P A V E D
P A T L A S C H O O L K H E
N G I S E D A O R L I A R D
K P T B X V T C A R T S B A
E Z O H O S P I T A L Y R H
Y L M O U N T A I N K T O S
G X T Z S S A P M O C N T D
R E L I E F L A C I T U A N
Z L D L T C H A W I Z O U E
L A E K D S N I T E T C Q G
E C G I T Y I A G I S Y E E
V S R R E V I R T H P T L L
A T E S L O B M Y S W A C U
R E E L F T R O P R I A C O
T Z S H I D E D I V I D Y I
D I R G O M H T U O S P A M
```

Solution on Page 334

BAKE

BLENDER

BREAD

BROIL

BURNER

CHILL

CHOP

CLEAVER

DICER

FAUCET

FLOUR

FOOD

FORK

FRUIT

FUNNEL

GRATER

GRILL

HEAT

JUICER

LADLE

LIGHTS

MALLET

MILK

OVEN

PANTRY

PEPPER

PLATES

SALT

SAUCE

SIFTER

SINK

SPICES

SPOONS

STIR

SUGAR

TASTE

TONGS

WARM

WHISK

YEAST

```
Y Y R T N A P R K L Y Z B C
C N R E P P E P L R D D Y S
R H B W D C C P I P O F E L
C H A A I N L Y M L O F A R
J R E D K T E C U A F D S O
M R A N S E A L S T L H T X
B I I G F R V H B E N E V O
O S N Q U B E U U S L A J S
O O C L N S R T B L S T T P
T A H R N N U O A U T P A O
J U I C E R O M I R H O S O
A T L R L S L M E L G H T N
S T L A S N F T S P I C E S
M M T I U R F G R I L L D Q
A J W W H I S K C Z Z P T R
E C U A S B T Q Q Y Y H A O
```

Solution on Page 334

AXIS

BED

BIT

BLADE

BOWLS

CARVING

CHISEL

CHUCK

CNC

CRAFT

CREATE

CUT

DESIGN

DRILL

ELECTRIC

FACTORY

FORMING

HEADSTOCK

KNURLING

LEGS

MACHINE

METAL

MOTOR

MOUNT

OPERATOR

PARTS

PATTERN

POTTERY

REDUCING

ROTATE

ROUND

SHAPE

SPIN

TAILSTOCK

TOOL

TURN

VISE

WHEEL

WOOD

WORKSHOP

```
M Z C T B Q V G S G E L V K
O E U I S L W O B H P N J H
U R T F A C T O R Y A T Y N
N T H A G N I M R O F P R R
T T A I L S T O C K K G E E
J E L E C T R I C N S E T T
T T B O I D D O J U V H T T
F A L P P U T E W R O A O A
A T A E C S W H S L X I P P
R O D R D A E T V I S E M Q
C R E A T E R F S N G A O N
H O E T L A L V Y G C N T R
U H S O P D S L I H G I O R
C D O R E D U C I N G P R Y
K T O B R O U N D R G S D C
C N C H I S E L P J D O O W
```

Solution on Page 334

ALMOND

BAKING

BURN

CALORIES

CANOLA

CHICKEN

COCONUT

CONSUME

COOK

CORN

DIET

EDIBLE

FAT

FIRE

FISH

FLAVOR

FOOD

FRY

GREASE

HEAT

HOT

KITCHEN

LIGHT

LIQUID

NUTRITION

OLIVE

PAN

PEANUT

PLANT

PRESS

RECIPE

REFINED

SALAD

SESAME

SMOKE

SOY

SPRAY

THICK

VIRGIN

YELLOW

Cooking Oil

```
D L F M E A J H F E B M B H
Y H S P R A Y D Y I A K R S
N P E E V I L O E L R E S I
A S T A P R H O V F C E O F
P L A N T G O F V I R G I N
Z T F U U C R V P P E C L A
E N S T O T K E A L M O N D
D E K O M S R I A L O N A C
I M K L Y B V I T S F S R O
B A K I N G C T T C E U E R
L S P G E F O U W I H M F N
E E Q H K H D N R M O E I P
H S J T C C A O B U R N N T
L I Q U I D L C W O L L E Y
C Z T Y H A A O M I J I D R
L T H I C K S C S L D Z W F
```

Solution on Page 334

ART

BLEACHED

BOX

BROWN

COATED

COLOR

CORRUGATED

CUT

FIBER

FOLD

GRADE

HEAVY

INDUSTRY

KRAFT

LAYERS

MAGAZINE

MATERIAL

MILL

PACKAGE

PAPER

PLY

PRESSED

PRINTING

PULP

RECYCLE

REUSE

RIGID

SHIPPING

SINGLE

STIFF

STRENGTH

STRONG

THICK

WEIGHT

WHITE

WOOD

WRITING

```
I Q B M P L L I M P U L P W
A O Y L E H L A I R E T A M
X R Y R E L G N I P P I H S
B I D E T A G U R R O C G S
N G N F Z S C N U G B Y U R
R I I I H S U H I K R A F T
F D N B R T C D E S O A X R
U E A E S Q G W N D W J D A
F T Y R P R I N T I N G E E
D A P A C K A G E T I H W T
L O R R E P A P E R O I G H
O C Y U E S X W R I T I N G
F Y V P C S U F F I T S O I
E U A Z L H S E C O L O R E
Z N E L C Y C E R U W G T W
H T H I C K W Y D O O W S P
```

Solution on Page 335

ANIMALS	POLES
AXE	PONCHO
BOOTS	RAFTING
CABIN	RAIN
CANTEEN	RETREAT
CLOTHES	ROPE
COOKING	SCOUTS
COOLER	SHELTER
CRAFTS	SKITS
DOME	SNOW
GLOVES	SOCKS
GRILL	STAKES
HAMMOCK	STOVE
HATCHET	SUMMER
HIKING	TENT
INSECTS	WEATHER
LANTERN	WINTER
LATRINE	WOODS
LOGS	
MATCHES	
NATURE	
PATH	

Solution on Page

```
H S T U O C S T N E T B N W
T J E A H L A E N X S S I E
A S U K T A S I H A O N V Q
E L N D A N R S S C T O O F
R A O I P T H T K E T U H W
T M G J A E S S R S L A R P
E I A L L R I U T O M O M E
R N G T O N E E M M P W P S
B A E F S V H H O M M E E Z
O R F E O C E C T S E H G G
O Y C T T H K S O A T R N L
T T A A I N C Q Z O E I T O
S F H X Y N A N L L K W K G
Y C L L I R G C O I J I T S
W O O D S I N O H P E D N O
R S T F A R C A B I N F F G
```

Solution on Page 335

ANTIQUE

BABY

BEND

BOWL

BRASS

CONCAVE

COOK

CUTLERY

DINNER

EAT

FEED

FLATWARE

FOOD

FORK

HANDLE

KITCHEN

KNIFE

LIQUID

MEDICINE

METAL

MIX

NAPKIN

OVAL

PLATE

PORCELAIN

REFLECTION

ROUND

SERVE

SETS

SILVER

SLURP

SOUP

SPOON

STAINLESS

STIR

SUGAR

TABLE

WOOD

```
J S R A S P D O O W U K M N
R B N L L Q K N T E R N I Y
Q Z S I L B B A U O V K X K
E A T Q A G B O F O P R E N
H G A U F L A T W A R E E Y
V A I I E M E R N L L H B S
T W N D E A E C O N C A V E
D P L D D V N D R T B E A T
P R E F L E C T I O N K K S
X U S I T E U K I C P E N D
H L S A M E T A L Q I K I P
F S L O V A L K S K U N F B
V P D I N N E R O O O E E I
R I T S S A R B U O I N K U
E N T N M I Y C P C D O O F
V L V Z N Y J S U G A R V D
```

Solution on Page 335

ATOMS

BLOCK

CEMENT

COLOR

CONCRETE

DENSE

DIAMOND

FILLED

FIRM

FORM

FREEZE

FROZEN

GLASS

GOLD

GRANITE

GROUND

HARD

ICE

IRON

LIQUID

MASS

MATERIAL

MATTER

METAL

MINERAL

OBJECT

OPAQUE

PACKED

PHASE

RIGID

ROCK

SCIENCE

STATE

STEEL

STONE

STURDY

TOUGH

VOLUME

WEIGHT

WOOD

Solid

```
W V W K K P H A S E N O T S
I N D N U O R G C S U D M P
V R N E R I G I D C A I H U K
K C O R T O U G H I N L C J
C L M N F I R M G E U O G D
O P A Q U E N F R N N Q O V
L Q I I C U C A R C Y O I O
B F D G R O L Y R E W M I L
Q F I L L E D E T G T A A U
T R X O C R T S N N T T O M
D E R S U E S A E O E B A E
M E X T U A S Z M M J C W M
V Z S A M T O S E E S N E D
N E O T E R P A C K E D A R
I J Z E F N O T H G I E W A
N D L O G W V F E T E M T H
```

Solution on Page 335

ARAK	LABNEH
ASIA	LAMB
COFFEE	MINT
CUISINE	OLIVES
CURRY	PARSLEY
DATES	PASTA
DIET	PERSIAN
DISH	PITA
DIVERSE	RICE
EAT	SALAD
FALAFEL	SAUCE
FIGS	SESAME
FOOD	SPICE
GARLIC	SUMAC
GREEK	SWEET
HONEY	SYRIAN
HUMMUS	TABLE
INDIA	TAHINI
JORDAN	
KEBAB	
KIBBEH	
KOFTA	

Middle Eastern Cuisine

```
H S W T N L E F A L A F Y A
D K V J E M I N T D B E A I
I O A F L H E B B I K L T N S
E R B C K T W V Z S A D S A
V A W O O Z E S R H I H P F
T A F F K R V A I A E U I O
F T Z F S C P N S J T M C O
A I P E R S I A N O Y M E D
D P H E N B A L L R L U I M
A A S G I F K I R D B S B J
F T L M R Q V U A A H Y N U
S E S A M E C G B N G R C M
E C U A S W E E Y P D I E T
L A M B P T K K S E T A D K
C V A Z A I S D P Y E N O H
R I C E T E X R E E C Z W K
```

Solution on Page 336

BATTERY

BOAT

CAR

CELL

CHARGE

CLEAN

COMMUTE

COST

DESIGN

DISTANCE

DRIVE

EFFICIENT

EMISSIONS

EXPENSIVE

FUEL

FUTURE

GREEN

HYBRID

MOTOR

NEW

NISSAN

OUTLET

PLUG

POLLUTION

POWER

PRIUS

QUIET

RANGE

SCOOTER

SMALL

SOLAR

SPEED

TAXES

TESLA

TORQUE

TOYOTA

TRAIN

TRUCK

VAN

VOLT

```
R J A A T M P F E R B E G B
A X S C O O T E R A E N R U
N N Z N K C U R T C V L E F
G M O T O R E T D R I V E U
E F F I C I E N T T S G N E
C B O A T R S O E E N A V L
N E X G Y U R S X R E W O P
A R I O L Q L A I L P E U N
T H R D U A T L C M X N J S
S E C E T U M M O C E N M D
I C N S G T L O V P B A Q T
D G Q I E R U T U F L S R P
C U U G A T A C E L L S R O
O L I N L R Q H Y B R I D A
S P E E D H T S C W U N G N
T A T O Y O T M Q S O L A R
```

Solution on Page 336

AIR

APPLIANCE

AUTOMOBILE

BLOW

BUILDING

BUTTONS

CAR

CENTRAL

CLIMATE

COILS

COLD

COMFORT

CONDENSER

CONTROL

COOL

DRY

DUCT

EFFICIENT

ENERGY

EXPENSIVE

FAN

FILTER

FREON

HEAT

HOT

HUMIDITY

HVAC

INDOOR

LUXURY

MACHINE

PORTABLE

POWER

PUMP

RELIEF

ROOM

SUMMER

SWITCH

SYSTEM

UNIT

VENT

Air Conditioning

```
H I B H F R E O N F D C V D
C P O C E N T R A L A L W T
T T M M G G N A I R E W O P
I C M U C N E T R O F M O C
W U A P P L I A N C E R H O
S D U R N M C D M R T U B O
M K T E M A I V L A M U L L
O C O T X O F G B I T N O U
O F M L M P F L D T U Q W X
R E O I A X E I O M H B C U
F I B F C D T N I N D O O R
K L I V H Y S Y S T E M N Y
Y E L H I V V C L I M A T E
R R E S N E D N O C V D R Y
C A V H E N E R G Y C E O C
T I N U Y T R Z A C O I L S
```

Solution on Page 336

AERIAL

BULLWHEEL

CABLE

CAPACITY

CARRY

CHAIR

ELECTRIC

ELEVATED

GEARBOX

HELP

HIGH

HILL

LIFT

LODGE

LOOP

MOTOR

MOUNTAIN

MOVEMENT

OPERATOR

PASSENGER

RAIL

RESORT

RIDE

ROPE

SAFETY BAR

SEAT

SIT

SKI

SLOW

SNOW

SPEED

STEEL

TERMINAL

TICKET

TOURIST

TOWER

TRANSPORT

VIEW

WINTER

WIRE

```
T E R M I N A L I F T B R J
H I L L L R A V I E W O N S
M O V E M E N T R N P M H T
Y B E L V C L I I E A O T E
U T U W E A A A O Q S T S K
S C E L E C T R I C I O I C
V H B H L N M E R R L R R I
E A G B U W H N D Y E E U T
C I J O I R H X J W G A O I
H R M N D L O E O N P S T K
S R T R A B Y T E F A S H S
G E G D O L X S A L O O P L
R R T R O P S N A R T E L O
A I C A P A C I T Y E M E W
I W D F P D T Y J D S P H B
L T A E S I T G E A R B O X
```

Solution on Page 336

ADDRESS

APARTMENT

BOX

BUSINESS

CARDS

CHUTE

COLLECT

CURBSIDE

DELIVER

DOOR

ENVELOPE

FLAG

FULL

HOME

HORIZONTAL

HOUSE

KEY

LETTER

MAGAZINES

MAIL

METAL

MOUNTED

OFFICE

OUTGOING

OUTSIDE

PACKAGE

PARCEL

POST

RECEIVE

RESIDENCE

RURAL

SAFE

SECURE

SEND

SLOT

STAMP

STEEL

STREET

USPS

VERTICAL

```
L M L E C R A P M A T S E S
A P E A E O D V V X G T Y X
T A T E P O L E V N E E C O
E C T M O A R O I L K E L N
M K E R O T R O A E B L D X
O A R L I U G T F R U P E O
H G G C L T N A M F S V L B
W E A A U O S T C E I X I F
S L R O Z E C S E E N C V M
F D U I L I A M C D E T E Y
W L R J E C N E D I S E R Q
C O A A D D R E S S S S P S U
H H L G C E D I S B R U C T
X O U T S I D E R U C E S T
H D S T R E E T I U O O R Q
J N D N E S L O T K P H M R
```

Solution on Page 337

ASCOT

BLOUSE

BLUE

BUSINESS

CASUAL

CLERIC

CLOTH

COAT

DRESS

EDWARDIAN

ELIZABETHAN

FABRIC

FLAT

FOLDED

GARMENT

HIGH

IRON

JACKET

LACE

LAPEL

LINEN

MAO

NECK

NOTCHED

OPEN

PIN

PRESSED

PRIEST

ROUND

SHIRT

STRAIGHT

STUDS

STYLE

SUIT

SWEATER

TIE

TUXEDO

WHITE

WIDE

WING

```
T L B U S I N E S S F F L D
T S E I R P A C J E T H N W
U S I L W H I T E X G Y I A
X E T E I R D C A N I D L N
E R Y P B Z R E I L E X T E
D D L A C E A W H R F N I P
O Y F L E I W B K C E N I O
F N P R D R D B E M T L L L
C O C E E H E G R T A O C C
Z R L A S T R A I G H T N T
I I O D S U G E D I B A S E
U A T T E C O H T N L T N K
M P H N R D O L L A U S A C
X W B P P I M T B D E O R A
B B Z H I G H R S L W W R J
R N G D N Y V S U I T R S I
```

Solution on Page 337

BALE	OATS
BARN	PACKAGING
BASKET	PACKING
BED	PAPER
BUILDING	PLANT
BUNDLE	RANCH
CATTLE	ROOF
CEREAL	ROPE
COB	SIP
CRAFTS	STALK
DRY	STEM
FARM	STUFFING
FEED	WHEAT
FIELD	
FOOD	
FUEL	
HAT	
HOLLOW	
HORSE	
HUT	
INSULATE	
LIVESTOCK	

```
J F R W L P W K E P O R K W
F F M A T E K S A B L S F L
B O F P N G I N S U L A T E
E O O P A C K A G I N G N L
E D C R V P H A V L B G U T
S D E B W L E E J D N B H T
R W C E S N S R Z I W A D A
O C R A F T S E K N H L R C
H O L L O W U C I G E E Y N
W Y S C I W A F S I A U G F
Q Y K H J P H T F T T F B E
F N M L L K E P U I A U V W
X R Z Y A M H B A R N O W Z
D C M K W T U H M D T G R L
E T W Q P I S K L A E R E C
Q M K E A M N E H O G O D N
```

Solution on Page 337

ACRYLIC

BEAUTY

BLACK

BOTTLE

BRIGHT

BRUSH

CHIPPED

CLEAR

COAT

COLOR

DECORATE

DRY

ENAMEL

ETHYL ACETATE

FILE

GEL

GIRLS

GLITTER

GLOSS

LACQUER

LIQUID

MAKEUP

NAILS

PAINT

PIGMENTS

PINK

PROTECT

RED

SALON

SHINE

SMELL

SPA

STRONG

STYLE

TEENS

TOE

VARNISH

WHITE

WOMEN

```
K I D G L T U L D U R Q T N
X W P E O T L A C Q U E R E
S W S T R O N G V Z T T A M
H Q L C I L Y R C A E A E O
I G S E H S I N R A V T L W
N L L T R O L O C Y O E C H
E P Y O N K C A L B O C O I
N L F R S E G P U E K A M T
A L I P D S M L B D C L I E
M Y S F P G Y G I H O Y O E
E L T T O B A U I T A H X N
L N Y U I N Q P H P T T C S
Z O L P A I P G S S N E M L
W L E I L E I A G I U E R E
S A L N D R B O A S L R I G
X S U K B R X P W L Y X B X
```

Solution on Page 337

ALE	IMPORTED
AMBER	INDUSTRY
ANHEUSER	KEG
BAR	LAGER
BEVERAGE	LIGHT
BOTTLE	MILLER
BRANDS	MUG
BREW	PABST
BUD	PARTY
CAN	PILSNER
COLD	PINT
COORS	PRODUCTION
CRAFT	PUB
DARK	REFRESHING
DOMESTIC	SCHLITZ
DRAFT	STOUT
DRINK	TAP
FLAVOR	YEAST
FOAM	
GRAIN	
HEAD	
HOPS	

```
V M P A T O D A E H X S Y R
O X D O E S M R R K D T M A
N V L B K B B E R K R O A A
O V U A E R G A N A C U O N
D D E R E A D I P Q I T F T
T G X L L N R I D M M X L S
G N L Y B D L O P U B L A A
U I I K A S R O O C D I V E
M H D P N D R A F T O G O Y
L S J E H T F A R C M H R E
U E R B E V E R A G E T L G
P R O D U C T I O N S T R D
E F A K S T J O A U T A L E
B E U W E R B C D O I O Y T
B R A Y R G S N B N C C W V
N G B S Z T I L H C S P O H
```

ARMY

AUTHORITY

AUTOCRACY

BUILDING

CITY

CONGRESS

CORRUPTION

COUNTRIES

DEBATE

DEMOCRATIC

DEPARTMENT

ECONOMY

ELECTIONS

IRS

LAWS

LEADERSHIP

LOBBYISTS

LOCAL

MAYOR

MUNICIPAL

OFFICIALS

OPPOSITION

PARLIAMENT

PEOPLE

POWER

PRESIDENT

PROTECTION

RULES

SENATORS

STATES

TAXES

THEOCRACY

VETO

VOTE

```
B C S E N A T O R S E L U R
U O V L O C A L S E T A T S
I U E E D V I E H L O W R N
L N T C O E R T O E F S E O
D T O T O G M B Y A F D W I
I R E I N N B O U D I E O T
N I C O T Y O T C E C P P P
G E C N I I H M M R I A A U
D S F S X O S U Y S A R R R
E V T R R P N O E H L T L R
B S I I E I F X P I S M I O
A U T O C R A C Y P I E A C
T Y P I O T Y M R A O N M T
E L P Y C A R C O E H T E C
E A A P R O T E C T I O N J
L M J K P R E S I D E N T Z
```

Solution on Page 338

ACCURACY

ALIGN

ANCIENT

ANGLE

ANTIQUE

AXIS

CIRCLE

CLOCK

DAY

DESIGN

DEVICE

DIAL

EARTH

EGYPTIAN

FACE

GARDEN

GNOMON

GREEK

HOUR

LATITUDE

LINES

METAL

MORNING

MOTTO

NOON

NORTH

NUMBERS

OBELISK

OLD

ORNAMENT

READING

ROMAN

ROUND

SCIENCE

SHADOW

STONE

STYLE

SUN

TIME

WATCH

Sundial

```
J T W R Y B D J W A F N A T
L T P L A H T R A E O A Q I
I A S H A D O W K C O L C C M
I L O T T O M I N S T Y L E
D A E I N B V S R E B M U N
N O R T H E L C R I C Q K O
U C G U D L M Q N G I S E D
O L X D L I S A E T D S G W
R S G E G S O T N E I C N A
A U N N G K E A O R W I I T
N X O A O Y T N L N O E D C
G G I H M M P S I A E N A H
L R I S D O O T U L T C E O
E E G L M O R N I N G E R F
W E O G A C C U R A C Y M W
L K A B J G A R D E N M P D
```

Solution on Page 338

BAKING

BLEND

BOTTLE

CAT

CEREAL

CHEESE

CHURN

COW

CREAMER

CUSTARD

DAIRY

DESSERT

DRINK

FAT

FOOD

FRESH

GRADES

HALF

HEAVY

ICE

INGREDIENT

LIGHT

LIQUID

LOTION

MILK

PIE

PURE

RISES

SAUCE

SHAVING

SKIM

SMOOTH

SOFT

SOUP

SWEET

TEA

TOP

WHEY

WHIP

YOGURT

```
Q W C D F Z K B I Z J Z G L
Y V H F S L Y K S S M I L K
R D D P A A A O C Y S N K U
D A Y I W T U H S V Q G M L
E I P O H P U C W A Q R A S
T R U G G R C H E E S E E N
N Y I Q N U I C E H R D D C
P L N H I I R Z T E A I R G
U P A F K L V T C R R E I E
R D S V A O F A G O A N N L
E I H M B T O C H M W T K T
V Y S L O I O D E S S E R T
M P E E M O D R A T S U C O
W N R H S N T J Z K O M A B
D X F M W U W H I P F E D D
X I F B S Z M M L G T O P K
```

Solution on Page 338

ALCOHOL

ALTERNATIVE

BIOMASS

CLEAN

CLIMATE

CONSERVATION

CORN

DAM

ECOLOGY

EFFICIENT

ELECTRIC

EMISSIONS

ENERGY

ENVIRONMENT

ETHANOL

FUEL

FUTURE

GLOBAL

GREEN

GRID

HEAT

HYDROGEN

INCENTIVE

INNOVATION

LIGHTING

NATURAL

POWER

RENEW

RESOURCE

SOLAR

SUN

TECHNOLOGY

THERMAL

TIDES

TURBINE

WATER

WIND

WOOD

```
Y G R E N E G O R D Y H D V
G F C L I M A T E Y O C N J
O U L E A I D I R G L O I T
L E E C L S L B B O I R W H
O L A T T S R I N L G N E E
C O N R E I E O E O H O C R
E N V I R O N M E N T I R M
V A U C N N E A R H I T U A
I H K S A S W S G C N A O L
T T R E T A W S D E G V S C
N E F F I C I E N T H O E O
E J P V V G L O B A L N R H
C O N S E R V A T I O N U O
N A T U R A L O S E D I T L
I K Z L E N I B R U T V U E
R E W O P T A E H D A M F N
```

Solution on Page 339

AMUSEMENT PARK

AUGUST

BARBEQUE

BASEBALL

BEACH PARTY

BIKING

BOATING

HIKING

ICE CREAM

JULY

JUNE

LEISURE

LEMONADE

OCEAN

PERSPIRATION

PICNIC

PLAYGROUND

POOL

POPSICLE

RELAX

ROCK CLIMBING

SLIDES

SNORKELING

SOCCER

SOFTBALL

SPRINKLERS

SUNGLASSES

TAN

TENNIS

TETHERBALL

TRIPS

VACATION

VOLLEYBALL

```
P O L L A B E S A B S O S O
S O C C E R U S I E L P C L
C I N C I P Q G X A L E R L
A M U S E M E N T P A R K A
G N I T A O B I S N N S T B
S E D I L S R B I G O P E Y
U P E S W X A M N K I I T E
N Z L M R U B I N C T R H L
G B C A G E L L E G A A E L
L T I U Y E L C T P C T R O
A S S K K G R K H V A I B V
S T P R I E R C N I V O A Y
S A O I A N A O J I K N L L
E N P M R E G R U U R I L U
S L L A B T F O S N N P N J
D P O O L E M O N A D E S G
```

Solution on Page 339

AIR

ANTENNA

ASSEMBLE

AVIATION

BATTERY

BUILD

CHANNELS

CONTROL

CRASH

DRONE

ELECTRIC

ENGINE

FAST

FIELD

FLY

FUN

GAS

GLIDER

HIGH

HOBBY

JOYSTICK

KIT

LANDING

MILITARY

MODEL

OUTSIDE

PARK

PLANE

RADIO

REMOTE

REPLICA

RUDDER

SCALE

SERVOS

SKY

SMALL

SPEED

TAKEOFF

TOY

WIND

```
P O U Y R E D D U R Z Z I Y
S A U O Y M C R E D I L G T
E R N T K I L P A R K B X F
R T A N S L L A B C A U F Y
V M O P E I C O N T R O L B
O D E M C T D S T D E A J B
S E N A E A N E I K I E S O
D G I N X R R A A R P N H H
A I G J O Y S T I C K O G G
P S N Y O I D A R G I R I X
M L E L E C T R I C T D H Z
Y O A Y F C H A N N E L S N
C M D N I W D L I U B F M U
T N W E E L A C S V A Z A F
V Q B E L B M E S S A G L X
M Q W F D I X A T N V Y L L
```

Solution on Page 339

ANIMALS

ANTIQUE

BENCH

CARNIVAL

CHILDREN

CIRCLE

DIZZY

FAIR

FAMILIES

FUN

GALLOPING

HORSE

KIDS

LIGHTS

LIONS

MARY POPPINS

MERRY

MIRRORS

MOVEMENT

MUSIC

OLD

ORGAN

PAINTED

PARK

PLATFORM

RIDE

RING

ROTATE

ROUND

SEAT

SPIN

TICKET

TIGERS

UNICORN

WOODEN

ZEBRAS

```
R P O O A B E X T Z D A O L
G T I C K E T C S Y E C M Y
W A N I M A L S R O R R I M
O P B E N C H G E L C R I C
O S R R M N A A G A T S E H
D E P S H E Z L I V N P E M
E A J P T N V L T I E A W F
N T P L L H I O P N R I U A
K H A A V I G P M R D N N I
B O R T G D O I S A L T I R
O R K F O P Y N L C I E C K
P S G O Y R Z G S Q H D O I
Z E B R A S Z N U F C R R D
K F A M I L I E S Z G I N S
F M U S I C D L O A C N V U
T Y E D I R O U N D S G S Z
```

Solution on Page 339

AMAZON

APPLE

AUTHOR

BATTERY

BOOK

CHAPTER

CHEAP

COLOR

COMPUTER

DATA

DEVICE

DIGITAL

DISPLAY

DOWNLOAD

EPUB

FICTION

FORMAT

FREE

HARDWARE

IMAGES

INTERNET

IPAD

KINDLE

LIBRARY

MEMORY

MOBILE

NOOK

NOVEL

ONLINE

PAGES

PDF

PUBLISH

READ

SCHOOL

SCREEN

SEARCH

SELL

SONY

TABLET

TEXT

Solution on Page

```
C D O L S L O O H C S A S F
L C P U B L I S H F Y T R H
I D O W N L O A D E R E F D
B X X M B I P P L C E X H A
R X D O P T I B E I T T N E
A I O I E U L U V V T T O R
R K N R G S T P O E A E O L
Y A L P S I D E N D B L K L
C U I F O O T R R X O B N E
M T N I N S E A H C R A E S
O H E C Y T T W L I D T E Y
B O B T N A T D K M P O R C
I R L I D F O R M A T O C H
L J N O Z A M A L G M D S E
E L D N I K P H D E L P P A
O W G M D G K I M S E G A P
```

Solution on Page 340

BARREL

BLACK

BLOTTER

CAP

CLASSIC

COLOR

CREATE

CURSIVE

DOCUMENT

DRAW

ELEGANT

FANCY

FILL

FLOW

FORMAL

GIFT

GOLD

GRAVITY

HAND

INK

LEAKAGE

LUXURY

MESSY

METAL

NIB

OFFICE

ORNATE

PARKER

PEN

QUALITY

QUILL

SCHOOL

SCRIPT

SHEAFFER

SIGN

STEEL

TIP

TOOL

WELL

WRITE

Fountain Pens

```
H N B U H U Z J D L S K A W
H W R Y V Z Y U E T U D N R
A L E C S T R E T T O L B I
I N U K L I S T B K C A L B T
D X R V L S E C U R S I V E
L U A S Z Y S M B I N D F U
O R P C S H E A F F E R A T
G Y X H P N R E L E G A N T
L L M O T R C O E C P W C P
C L A O E I O R A T Q H Y I
H O I L F T P T K U A M N R
D I R F F O R M A L W E M C
C Z O N I Y W L G I F T R S
W H G P A P I O E R O L O C
J I Q L A T E M L L I U Q G
S K G X Y C E N H F Q E P L
```

Solution on Page 340

AQUA

ARID

CANAL

CHANNELS

CORN

CROP

DAM

DITCH

DRY

EMITTERS

FARM

FIELD

FLOW

FLUSHING

FOOD

GARDEN

GREEN

GROW

HARVEST

HOSE

LAND

LAWN

PIPE

PRODUCE

PUMP

RAIN

RICE

RIVER

RUNOFF

SCIENCE

SOIL

SPRAY

SUPPLY

SURFACE

SYSTEM

TRENCH

TROUGH

VALVES

WATER

YARD

```
N F Y F L H A Y M I F P D I
C R O P A O P P F A R M S K
D S O S W S E V L A V U L Z
V L H C N E R T U T D P W E
Y E M I T T E R S N R F T H
V N Y E F X R E H E A I C J
U N E N W I V C I D Y E Q H
R A Y C V R L U N R C L A G
E H A E A E I D G A G D R A
C C R H D C O O F G F O I L
I O P V P O S R F L W N D Q
R N S A F I U P O A F E I C
A E K U K S P W N N A E T B
I K T Q B P P E U D V R C E
N C C A N A L T R O U G H X
J S O O W S Y S T E M A D B
```

Solution on Page 340

AMBASSADOR

AMERICA

AUTHOR

AUTOBIOGRAPHY

BALD

CONSTITUTION

CREATIVE

CURRENCY

DELEGATE

EDITOR

ELECTRICITY

EXPERIMENT

FATHER

FOUNDING

GLASSES

GREAT

INDEPENDENCE

KITE

NEWSPAPER

PATRIOT

PENNSYLVANIA

PENNY SAVED

PHILADELPHIA

POOR RICHARD

PRESIDENT

PRINTER

SCIENTIST

STOVE

USA

WASHINGTON

WIT

Ben Franklin

```
D E L E G A T E R O H T U A
F A T H E R C R E A T I V E
D N E L E C T R I C I T Y X
Y H P A R G O I B O T U A P
P R D E V A S Y N N E P N E
R E G Y A M B A S S A D O R
E P N C S C I E N T I S T I
S A I N E A M E R I C A G M
I P D E S P R I N T E R N E
D S N R S Y O O A U B N I N
E W U R A T L R T T A K H T
N E O U L S O V A I L I S A
T N F C G X U V A O D T A E
I N D E P E N D E N C E W R
W A I H P L E D A L I H P G
O W H P O O R R I C H A R D
```

Solution on Page 340

AISLE

BEST MAN

BOUQUET

CANDLES

CHAPEL

CHURCH

COUPLE

DANCING

DINNER

DRESSES

EVENT

FAMILY

FATHER

FOOD

FORMAL

FRIENDS

GARTER

GIFTS

GOWN

GUESTS

HUSBAND

KISS

LAW

LOVE

MOTHER

MUSIC

PRIEST

RICE

RINGS

RITUALS

SHOWER

SPEECH

TOAST

TUXEDO

UNION

VEIL

VIDEO

VOWS

WHITE

WIFE

```
N W O G I F T S H C E E P S
V F I A M W W U L W H I T E
E V C F L U S T S A O T F Q
I V V H E B S S I K U W A L
L F E D A N C I N G J T M H
N O I N U P A T C S R E I P
I O D M T C E M N E L U L R
R D Z S H L E L T S O Q Y I
E F X U P L K R R S V U O E
W V R U S T A G E E E O P S
O C O I R G U L F R N B U T
H C A I E E D X A D I N L S
S M C S S N H Q E M S N I U
R E H T A F D T Q D R M G D
K A S C I I A S O W O O G S
S W O V I D E O P M O Y F K
```

Solution on Page 341

ALARM

APRIL

ATOMIC

AUGUST

BEAT

BIG BEN

CENTURY

CUCKOO

DAY

DECADE

DECEMBER

DIGITAL

ELECTRIC

FALL

FEBRUARY

FORTNIGHT

HANDS

HOURS

JANUARY

JULY

JUNE

MAY

MINUTES

MOMENT

MONTH

NOVEMBER

OCTOBER

PENDULUM

QUARTZ

SEASON

SECONDS

STRIKE

SUMMER

SUNDIAL

TIMER

TOWER

WALL

WATER

WEEK

WINTER

```
P S R V Q U A R T Z E Y I H
N D E C A D E F Z K L N J O
G N W S O B A S I U E A O U
A A O E O L E R J B N U O R
L H T T L C T C G U F G K S
A A C U O S W I A O E U C U
R O T N A U B R R X B S U M
M O D I S N Y T E T R T C M
O S C M G D N C B N U I E E
N E I O Y I T E M E A M N R
T A M T G A D L E M R E T E
H S O H E L M E C O Y R U T
L O T B I N O V E M B E R N
L N A R M U L U D N E P Y I
A A P S N F K E E W U N A W
W A T E R U J V A F D J D X
```

Solution on Page 341

ACRES

APPRAISAL

ASSETS

BOAT

BUY

CAR

CONTROL

DEED

FARM

FENCE

HOME

HOUSE

LAW

LEASE

LEGAL

LIBERTY

LIEN

LOT

MINE

MONOPOLY

MORTGAGE

MOVABLE

OWN

PERSONAL

POSSESS

PRIVATE

PUBLIC

PURCHASE

REAL

RENT

RIGHT

SELL

TAX

THINGS

TITLE

TRACT

TRUST

VALUE

WEALTH

WILL

```
H I F L T A W S Z W D N H X
N B D P S R S E B E W D W T
Z V E S H E A E A O D I A Y
X Q E E S O U C E L A X L I
T T D S R L M N T L T T T L
S M O V A B L E V Q T H I A
Z P C V C H G F N P T I X S
T Y Z R A L C M E R L N T I
E T A C D M O R T G A G E A
O R R Y R N S R U R E S T R
G E U A O O L B T P R H A P
S B F P N L B T U N G H V P
L I O A A E E B R I O J I A
J L L G L N L A R U F C R A
Y N E I L I O B S M S V P A
T L J S C M T E S E W T A D
```

Solution on Page 341

APPLE

BALLS

BRACELET

CANDY CANE

COAL

COFFEE

COLOGNE

COSMETICS

CRAYONS

DOLL

DVD

FRUIT

GAG GIFT

GAMES

GIFT CARDS

GUM

IPOD

LIPSTICK

LOTION

MONEY

NAIL POLISH

NECKLACE

NUTS

ORANGES

PENCILS

PERFUME

PUZZLE

SHAMPOO

SNOW GLOBE

SOAP

STICKERS

TEA

TOOTHBRUSH

TOYS

UNDERWEAR

WATCH

```
E J M L I P S T I C K X X P
M O N E Y L S H A M P O O K
U U X V I E E N G O L O C W
F N G C M D D L A O C Z O A
R D N A S Y O T T S F T F T
E E G M C T E L N C F A F C
P R N A I L P O L I S H E H
S W N O E U W W G T D S E C
L E N C Z G P G T E R U U W
L A A Z L A A I I M A R C Q
A R L O O G S H U S C B R P
B E B S E G N A R O T H A A
N E C K L A C E F C F T Y S
N U D O P I E A F M I O O S
M V T E P D Q T E F G O N L
D O S S A S R E K C I T S T
```

Solution on Page 341

ACTION

ARCADE

ATARI

BUTTON

CARTRIDGE

CHEATS

COMPUTER

CONSOLE

CONTROLS

DEVICE

DISC

FUN

GAME

GRAPHICS

HANDHELD

JOYSTICK

JUMP

KEYBOARD

LEVEL

MMORPG

MOUSE

MUSIC

NINTENDO

ONLINE

PLAY

PONG

RACING

RATINGS

REMOTE

SCREEN

SHOOTER

SONY

SOUND

SPORTS

STRATEGY

SYSTEM

TETRIS

VIOLENCE

WII

XBOX

Electronic Games

```
G N O P V F H X O B X F S L
O N P D D I U Y C A T A R I
W I I E N I L N O I T C A D
U S M C N I N T E N D O T E
C A R C A D E C N E L O I V
G D S P O R T S J A E R N I
U R O M Y M N O R M H E G C
V A U U G U Y W M E D T S E
Y O N J E S L O R T N O C T
A B D S T I S S E S A O Y O
L Y U I A C I T T Y H H N M
P E C T R R M O U S E S O E
A K V E T G R A P H I C S R
D Z E E S O K M M O R P G R
J N T O L A N C O N S O L E
E G D I R T R A C H E A T S
```

Solution on Page 342

AIR

ANIMAL

BEHAVIOR

BIOME

BIRDS

BOTANY

CARBON

CLIMATE

COMMUNITY

DIVERSITY

EARTH

ECOLOGIST

ECOSPHERE

ECOSYSTEM

ENERGY

EVOLUTION

FOOD WEB

FORESTRY

GENETICS

GLOBAL

HABITAT

HUMAN

LIFE

LIVING

MIGRATION

NATURE

NICHE

OCEAN

ORGANISM

PLANT

RECYCLE

RELATIONS

SCIENCE

SOCIAL

SOIL

SPECIES

STUDY

TREES

WEATHER

```
L M B U I T N A L P J M F T
I S D R I B L I F E I F O R
O I B S L A B O L G S O R E
S N O I T A L E R N C O E E
E A B N O B R A C I I D S S
I G E D O M T R M V T W T E
C R C C I I E T A I E E R H
E O O Y O V T H K L N B Y C
P E S N I L E U U S E A R I
S N P A Q B O R L M G I E N
R E H T A E W G S O A R T A
Y R E O C E A N I I V N A T
D G R B E C O S Y S T E M U
U Y E C O M M U N I T Y I R
T A T I B A H R E C Y C L E
S S L A I C O S C I E N C E
```

Solution on Page 342

AUTOMATIC

BLACK

BOOKS

COLOR

COMPUTER

COPY

DIGITAL

DOCUMENT

DRUM

DUPLEX

EDUCATION

ELECTRIC

EXPOSURE

FAX

GLASS

GOVERNMENT

HEAT

IMAGE

INK

JAM

LETTER

LIBRARY

LIGHT

MECHANICAL

MULTIPLE

NUMBER

OFFICE

PAGES

PAPER

PHOTO

PROCESS

QUICK

ROLLER

SCAN

SCHOOL

TONER

TRAY

WHITE

WORK

XEROX

```
Y Z X K F A E T R K C I U Q
G A R R E L L O R B O O K S
F O R E N D L T O N E R M S
W H I T E O E X P O S U R E
A N N T C U D I G I T A L C
K S U E F U G E S T T M O O
T C M L P C O P Y A E U O R
H A B L I C V R C C D L H P
V N E V T B E I H U O T C I
P X R H B T R A X D C I S E
G A G K U T N A O E U P O G
B I P P C I M S R X M L F L
L S M E C D E Q E Y E E F A
A O L A R G N L X J N I I S
C E L U A U T O M A T I C S
K R M P H O T O I M A G E U
```

Solution on Page 342

BIG

BUILDING

CHICAGO

CITY

COMMUNITY

CONCRETE

DECORATED

DRINK

ELEVATED

FILL

FLOW

GRAVITY

HEIGHT

HIGH

HILL

LADDER

LANDMARK

LARGE

LEAK

METER

MONUMENTS

MUNICIPAL

PAINT

PIPE

PRESSURE

PUMP

RAIN

ROOFTOP

ROUND

SAFETY

SIGN

STEEL

STORAGE

SUPPLY

TAP

TOWN

USAGE

VOLUME

WATER

WELL

Water Tower

```
W A T E R K I H W E L L C S
O R O O F T O P H I G H I Y
L S U S T O R A G E I G J K
F N M E E E T E R C N O C R
D Y V E S M B R A I N D O A
U S T S Y I U G D R I N K M
E F U I G T O L A R G E D D
H R S P N R I P O P L L E N
E E A Y P U A C I V A T T A
I D G T B L M V V P A O A L
G D E E Q O Y M I R E W V E
H A L F P C M C O T U N E E
T L L A U E I C X C Y P L T
A U I S T N E M U N O M E S
P N F E U D L L I H V U A U
T X R M J K H O D N J P K A
```

Solution on Page 342

ACTIVITY

AGILITY

ATHLETIC

BENEFITS

BODY

BREATHING

CARBOHYDRATES

CATABOLIC

CYCLING

DIET

ENDORPHINS

ENDURANCE

EXERTION

EXHALATION

FITNESS

FLEXIBILITY

GYM

HEALTHY

HIKING

JOGGING

MARATHON

MUSCLES

OBESITY

RUNNING

SHAPE

SKILLS

SPORTS

SPRINTING

STRETCHING

SWEAT

SWIMMING

WALKING

WATER

```
S P R I N T I N G Y M F H M
W E Y G N I G G O J Y I D U
A C T I V I T Y T H K T F S
L N I A T H L E T I C N K C
K A L G R B I L N F G E C L
I R I N Z D A G N L N S I E
N U G I B E Y O E E I S L S
G D A H H R I H X X N E O W
M N O C E T S H O I N J B I
A E L T R P A T H B U W A M
R L A E O L A P W I R V T M
A W X R A E R H I L D A A I
T E T T W O B E S I T Y C N
H S I S D B R E A T H I N G
O O G N I L C Y C Y D O B E
N B E N E F I T S L L I K S
```

Solution on Page 343

AUTUMN	ORANGE
BLADE	OXYGEN
BLOWER	PALM
BOTANY	PARK
BRANCH	PILE
BROWN	PLANT
CHANGE	RAKE
COLOR	RED
CRUNCHY	SEASON
DRY	SHADE
FALL	SPRING
FERNS	TABLE
FLAT	TEA
FOLIAGE	THIN
FOOD	TWIG
GOLD	VEIN
GRASS	WIND
GROW	YELLOW
LIGHT	
MAPLE	
MULCH	
OAK	

```
O D W R D M C U T A L F B S
A F G H L Q H A C N G Z E R
K E P F S V B O N E A E D R
G R O W Y L L E A B L L A F
N N A B E O G R A S S P P A
E S M P R Y W E E G N A R O
D B H U X A T I G D T M Q R
N T B O T A N Y N O S A E S
V Y H C N U R C A D K D D H
Q R C I S B A F H C M S A A
C D Y K N F L O C R U G L D
V K U E D N W O R B L J B E
V R P A L M P D W I C I K X
Y K I F O L I A G E H A B L
L G L Q G B O H S P R I N G
B V E I N G T W I G G B K N
```

Solution on Page 343

APPETIZERS

APPLE CRISP

BERRY PIE

BRANDY SNAPS

BROWNIES

CANDY CANES

CARAMEL

CHEESECAKE

CHERRY PIE

CHESTNUTS

CIDER

FUDGE

HARD CANDY

ICE CREAM

KISSES

MACAROONS

MARSHMALLOW

MIXED NUTS

PECAN PIE

PEPPERMINT

PICKLES

PUMPKIN PIE

PUNCH

ROCK CANDY

SHORTBREAD

SODA

SPONGE CAKE

TOFFEE

VEGGIE DIP

```
T R S H O R T B R E A D O S
N E I P Y R R E H C N U P C
I D F W O Y D N A C D R A H
M I X E D N U T S F U D G E
R C S B V E G G I E D I P E
E R T R A P P E T I Z E R S
P O U A P P L E C R I S P E
P C N N E B S I A A S M U C
E K T D C R N P N C K A M A
P C S Y A O O Y D A I E P K
I A E S N W O R Y R S R K E
C N H N P N R R C A S C I E
K D C A I I A E A M E E N F
L Y S P E E C B N E S C P F
E X V S T S A L E L B I I O
S W O L L A M H S R A M E T
```

Solution on Page 343

ADVICE

CALL

CAPSULES

CHEMISTRY

COSMETICS

COUNTER

DISPENSE

DOCTOR

DOSE

DRUG

FILL

GENERIC

HEALTH

HOSPITAL

INSURANCE

LICENSED

MORTAR

NURSE

ORDER

PATIENT

PESTLE

PHARMACIST

PHYSICIAN

RETAIL

SAFE

SCIENCE

SERVICE

SICKNESS

STORE

SUBSTANCE

TABLET

THERAPY

TRAINING

TREATMENT

VITAMINS

WALGREENS

WELLNESS

```
G M O R T A R T E L B A T D
U P R O E S R U N Q Y I U O
R A D T S I C A M R A H P S
D T E C A L L I T S T O R E
D I R O S U B S T A N C E L
W E S D S A I C T E E H V U
E N S P N M F I R C M O I S
L T S N E A D E A N T S C P
L H I H E N I N I A A P O A
N E C E R C S C N R E I U C
E R K A G E I E I U R T N I
S A N L L I F L N S T A T R
S P E T A M R T G N Y L E E
G Y S H W R E T A I L H R N
C E S N I M A T I V V P P E
P S E R V I C E C I V D A G
```

Solution on Page 343

AUDIBLE	HOUR
BEN	KREMLIN
BRICK	LANDMARK
BUILDING	LARGE
CAMPUS	LONDON
CANTERBURY	MINUTES
CATHEDRAL	MONUMENT
CENTRAL	NOON
CHIME	OLD
CHURCH	RING
CITY	SQUARE
CLOCK	STAIRS
DESIGN	STRIKING
DIAL	STRUCTURE
ENGLAND	TALL
ERECTED	TIME
FACE	TOWN
FAMOUS	TURRET
GEARS	
HAND	
HEIGHT	
HIGH	

```
R W L C H U R C H A N D M I
I C V L F A M O U S I O Z I E
O S A W T N E M U N O M N G
T A T E M I T J D K N G U N
H O U R A S N E C M L N T I
K D B D U G T I R A X I E D
C A I P I C R Y N B F K S L
O A M S E B T D O A U I A I
L A E R H I L U C L N R M U
C D E E C F A E R N D T Y B
X L O N D O N G I E S S C R
T E R R U T D L H B R G C T
S Q U A R E M T H G I E H N
E G R A L E A O I N A A I N
Z A L R R C R W G I T R M R
T C D K N L K N H R S S E G
```

Solution on Page 344

ALUMINUM

BAGS

BATTERIES

BOTTLES

CANS

CARDBOARD

CENTER

CLEAN

COLLECTION

COMPOSTING

CONSUMPTION

CURBSIDE

DEPOSIT

EARTH

ECOLOGY

EFFICIENCY

ELECTRONICS

ENERGY

FOOD

GLASS

GREEN

INDUSTRY

LANDFILLS

MATERIALS

METAL

NEWSPAPERS

PACKAGING

POLLUTION

PROCESSING

RESOURCES

REUSE

SCRAP

SORTING

STEEL

```
N E W S P A P E R S C R A P
G A L U M I N U M E T A L L
L H E E D I S B R U C B P A
A T F S C O L L E C T I O N
S R F M A T E R I A L S L D
S A I C S O R T I N G P L F
E E C B O V D O O F R R U I
N O I T P M U S N O C O T L
E B E R D E P O S I T C I L
R R N C E Y G O L O C E O S
G V C E N T E R S L O S N E
Y B Y L E E T S E T G S E L
D R A O B D R A C A I I E T
Y R T S U D N I B A X N R T
J P W P A C K A G I N G G O
S E C R U O S E R E U S E B
```

Solution on Page 344

BELTWAY

BICYCLES

BRAKING

BRIDGE

BYPATH

BYROAD

CAR SEAT

CAUSEWAY

COASTING

CROSSWALK

CRUISING

CURVES

DETOUR

DOWNSHIFT

DRIVEWAY

FREEWAY

FUEL

GREEN

HIGHWAY

HILLS

INSURANCE

LANE

MAIN ROAD

MIRRORS

PARKWAY

RACING

REST STOP

ROADWAY

SHORTCUT

SPEEDING

SPEEDWAY

TRAFFIC

TURNOFF

TURNPIKE

YELLOW

YIELD

```
N V B F S R O R R I M T O F
B J Y R P E K I P N R U T F
P S P E E D I N G V L C R O
A E A E E B R I D G E T A N R
R V T W D G N I S I U R C R
K R H A W P N B V A F O I U
W U T Y A O D I R E X H N T
A C R T Y T E C T A W S G N
Y W A F I S T Y A S K A K E
A O F I E T O C A R A I Y E
W L F H L S U L B W S O N R
H L I S D E R E H Y T E C G
G E C N A R U S N I R L A G
I Y A W E S U A C A L O E T
H C R O S S W A L K L L A B
Y A W D A O R N I A M D S D
```

Solution on Page 344

BED
BLANKET
BOLSTER
CASE
CHAIR
COMFORT
COUCH
COVER
CUSHION
DECOR
DESIGN
DOWN
DREAM
FEATHER
FIGHT
FIRM
FLUFFY
FOAM
HARD
HEAD
KING
LACE

LINEN
NAP
NECK
NIGHT
QUEEN
RELAX
REST
SATIN
SILK
SLEEP
SLIP
SOFA
STANDARD
SUPPORT
THROW
TOP
TRAVEL
WHITE

Solution on Page

```
L X N F K L I S K Q T F Z N
Y E A R H I J O Z O S O F A
Z X P L S T N E P O E Y M P
W H I T E L R G T H R F Z A
E B P S J R E H T A E F E H
Q D A T R A V E L R V U Y S
U C R Q D K K R P D O L L H
E D W E R N V R O M C F A E
E T B D A E W D H C O U C H
N R Q L D M T E A O E A E F
E O B U N U A S C M C D W X
C P I C A D M I L F I G H T
K P N H T D A G I O M H Q G
F U Z A S J O N N R B R A D
D S L I P U F W E T H G I N
O T H R O W C E N I T A S F
```

Solution on Page 344

AISLES

ANNOUNCER

ARENA

AUDIENCE

BALL

BAND

BEER

BUILDING

CHEERS

CITY

CONCERT

EVENT

FANS

FIELD

FOOD

HOCKEY

HUGE

INDOOR

LARGE

LIGHTS

LIVE

MUSIC

OPEN

OUTDOOR

PARK

PEANUTS

PEOPLE

PLAY

POPCORN

ROWS

SCORE

SEAT

SECURITY

SOCCER

SPORT

STAGE

SUITES

TEAM

TICKET

TRACK

Stadium

```
T R O P S E E G A T S Z S L
R N T E O Y G U E J T S J N
A F E P C T D A P A H T B J
C A E V C I M O T I G U N P
K N N V E C P I Y S I N L M
R S S N R C C Y E L L A B R
B Y C R O K C A D E Y E A Z
L E I R E U N I D S C P N C
F K N T N E N D S O F N D G
S C D D R G H C N U O S B S
W O O A L P V C E F M F Y U
O H O A K S E C U R I T Y L
R K R A P R O O D T U O I C
E G S E T I U S P Y Q V Y B
E R O C S E A T D L E I F J
B T H U F G K H U G E D H S
```

Solution on Page 345

PUZZLES • 261

BLOCK

CANADA

CASCADE

CATARACT

CHANNEL

CHUTE

CLIFF

CURRENT

DROP

ENERGY

EROSION

FAN

FLOW

FROZEN

GOCTA

GORGE

HAWAII

HEIGHT

LAKE

MIST

NATURE

NIAGARA

PARK

PLUNGE

POOL

RAINBOW

RAPID

RELAXING

RIVER

ROCKS

ROMANTIC

SCENIC

SPLASH

SPRAY

STEEP

STREAM

TALL

TIERED

WATER

WET

```
K V A Y R G P L W O L F D V
L R A S A O S A L Z C F Y B
D S F A R R C T R A I I X F
I E I D I G P K R K T L E D
P W D A I E T S S E N C N E
A E U N A D G N I X A L E R
R T B A W A I L E T M M R O
E I C C A C R A A R O J G S
T E U O H S R R F K R Y Y I
A R T Q G A A A R W E U X O
W E H W G C N I O K V N C N
P D G A T Y V N Z C I H I A
Y E I N A F Q B E O R L N T
K N E T U H C O N L X O E U
W W H T T L W W O B V O C R
S Z M I S T P H S A L P S E
```

Solution on Page 345

ABILITY	PEN
ACE	PHYSICAL
ANSWER	PREPARE
APTITUDE	PROCTOR
BOOKS	QUESTION
CHEAT	QUIZ
CLASS	READING
COMPUTER	RESULT
EASY	SAT
EVALUATE	SCHOOL
EXAM	SCIENCE
FAIL	SCORE
FALSE	SKILL
GED	STUDY
GRE	TEST
HARD	TIMED
LEARN	TRUE
MATH	WRITTEN
MEMORY	
MILITARY	
ORAL	
PASS	

Testing, Testing

```
T S E T O E Y T R B Q V R B
E E R L K D D E O M T O E W
N S O W U E W O M A T H S Q
Q L C T M S K U S C T R U E
Y A S I N S C H O O L I L U
I F T A E E D R A H Z X T G
J T M R T N P H Y S I C A L
Q L G Y T E C E R A P E R P
R I S R I T R E A A Q J O M
D A P O R A T Y T I L I B A
E F L M W U C S I L L C T X
G D A E P L S V L L M H F E
X I R M A A G N I D A E R Q
X A O S P V K K M N R A E L
W C S Q U E S T I O N T M V
H E E D U T I T P A O Y P G
```

Solution on Page 345

BADGE

CAMPAIGN

CERAMIC

CLOSURE

COAT

COLLAR

COVERED

CUTE

DESIGN

DRESS

FABRIC

FASTEN

FLY

GARMENT

GLASS

HOLE

JACKET

JEANS

KNOB

LOOP

PANTS

POCKET

PUSH

ROUND

SEW

SHANK

SHIRT

SHORTS

SIZE

SKIRT

SNOWMAN

STUD

SUIT

SWEATER

Cute as a Button

```
L C A M P A I G N C L D W E
G D E S I G N H O L E N R G
S K I R T G I A P P S U O D
G Y L F A S T E N C S O X A
U M B B H M B T P O E R Y B
Q O S A O S I G L V R U M S
K W N F H N L C A E D C J T
I K B I L A K Y Z R I U R R
K P R O S E L I A E M T B O
G T O S T J S L F D S E W H
B P L C E U L N A M W O N S
E U J Q K O H F B P E E S T
G S C P C E M W R A A H U U
P H U X A I T Q I V T N I D
Q X A K J Y U I C V E A T V
O I N K O Z Q X Q R R D U S
```

Solution on Page 345

ALARMS	OXYGEN
ARSON	PUMP
AXE	RADIO
BELL	RAIN
BLAZE	RAKE
BURN	RANGER
CAMPERS	RESCUE
COALS	SAFETY
CPR	SEARCH
DRY	SHOVEL
FOAM	SIREN
FUEL	SPARKS
GEAR	TEAM
GLOVES	TORCH
GREASE	WATER
HEAT	WIND
HELMET	WIRING
HORN	WOOD
HOSES	
LADDER	
MASK	
OIL	

```
O C X S H Y S P A R K S B S
T T U Z T C C L X F E X D K
F K T E A M A X T U P E F I
J S F P S R M F C E S X Q F
F D A U C M A P S R L H A G A
S M H S P Y E K A R O R F D
P W E T N R R R N E V S E B
N G L O V E S D G Z E O D O
R N M R Y D G G E A L N O I
G I E C P D E Y R L I O O E
C R T H C A E C X B H M W M
N I A R R L H L O O H A L P
H W E D R D D L S A T O R F
D U H M I R N E L E L F R Q
H K X H D O S I R E N S H N
E R G W X H G Z W X B U R N
```

Solution on Page 346

ACCORD

AFFECTION

AFFINITY

BEHAVIOR

BONDING

BUDDIES

CHILDHOOD

CHILDREN

CLOSENESS

COLLEGE

CONFIDANT

DEPEND

EMOTIONAL

EMPATHY

FAMILY

FEELING

FOREVER

FRIENDS

HELP

HONESTY

IMPORTANT

INTIMACY

JOY

LOVE

LOYALTY

MARRIAGE

NEED

PARTNER

RESPECT

ROMANCE

ROOMMATE

SCHOOL

SHARING

SYMPATHY

TOGETHER

TRUE

```
J Y G T R U E T A M M O O R
R E H T E G O T F A M I L Y
O X T T E D Y I R G Y O J S
M R R L A T E R I N C N S E
A D L E L P I E E I O E C I
N O O A V A M Y N L N R H D
C R Y O G E D Y D E F D O D
E O D E H I R E S E I L O U
L I A R M D M O P F D I L B
G V F H O O L P F E A H B R
N A F F E C T I O N N N C O E
I H I T D L C I H R T D N S
R E N T R A P A O C T V D P
A B I Y C A M I T N I A I E
H Y T S E N O H L A A Y N C
S O Y H T A P M E V O L G T
```

Solution on Page 346

AISLES

APPLES

BAGS

BAKERY

BANANAS

BANKING

BEER

BOOKS

BREAD

BULK

CANNED

CART

CASHIER

CHEESE

CHIPS

CLERK

COOKIES

COUPONS

DAIRY

DELI

EGGS

FILM

FLOWERS

FRESH

FRUIT

JAM

JUICE

MEAT

MILK

PASTA

RICE

SALE

SNACKS

SOAP

SODA

SPICES

SWEETS

VIDEOS

WINE

YOGURT

```
Y H Q J A J B E P G Q P F W
I Z B O O K S P D A I R Y I
X N I A M E G G S C E Q O N
P B A N K I N G A S V H G E
C A S H I E R O H B I T U L
O N S L Z F R U I T D A R A
O A P T T Q Q Y S W E E T S
K N K F A R M L E G O M E Z
I A O L P B A A U M S C H P
E S N O P U O C J U I C E A
S M I W L E B F A P Z L S O
M K C E E S K D S N A C K S
H L H R S E A D O S N R W Q
V A I S L E S C E R E E B S
E B P F R H F B U L K V D Y
G U S B H C R I C E I G Z L
```

Solution on Page 346

BASIN

BATH

BOTTOM

BOWL

CERAMIC

CHROME

CLEAN

CLOG

COMET

COPPER

COUNTER

DESIGN

DIRTY

DISHES

DOUBLE

DRAIN

ENAMEL

FAUCET

FILL

FIXTURE

GLASS

GRANITE

HANDS

HEAVY

HYGIENE

KITCHEN

MARBLE

MODERN

PIPE

RINSE

SCRUB

SOAP

SPONGE

STEEL

STONE

SUDS

TAP

TOWEL

WASH

WATER

```
H S A W L S X G O L C S H T
A B R E D U Y B H O P C P G
N U E D R D A G M O B R I V
D T J K A S D E N O A U P B
S E H S I D T G W J O B E G
M D I N N T E L B R A M L X
C E M O R H C O P P E R B Z
S S A L G I U H M N J B U B
O I I C I M A R E C X A O S
A G Z L O H F I W N E T D T
P N T E E U G I F R T H M O
R E T A W Y N S U O I F O W
A S V N H O T T M T N Q D E
H Y K V S O X R E N A M E L
X W E S N I R I I I R R P R S
I K V E F I L L W D G C N N
```

Solution on Page 346

ART

BRANDING

BUILDINGS

CHICAGO

COUNTRIES

CULTURE

DESIGN

EDUCATION

EIFFEL TOWER

EPCOT

EXCHANGE

EXHIBIT

EXPO

FERRIS WHEEL

FESTIVAL

FUN

GAMES

INDUSTRY

INNOVATION

INVENTIONS

KNOXVILLE

LONDON

MONTREAL

NATIONS

NEW YORK

PAVILION

PEOPLE

RIDES

SCIENCE

STRUCTURES

TECHNOLOGY

THEME

UNIVERSAL

WORLD

```
R I N D U S T R Y S E M A G
I E H Y N G N I D N A R B A
D N W G O N E E E O T C T I
E T O O I I L M S I C O E A
S O R L T D P E I T U U C Z
C C L O A L O H G N L N N F
H P D N V I E T N E T T E K
I E P H O U P F D V U R I Z
C L A C N B N U F N R I C L
A L V E N B C L I I E E S A
G I I T I A O V S O E S N V
O V L Q T N E W Y O R K O I
P X I I D R H E X H I B I T
X O O O S E R U T C U R T S
E N N A E X C H A N G E A E
J K L L A E R T N O M Q N F
```

ALUMINUM

BARBED

BATTERY

BEND

BRAIDED

BUNDLE

CABLE

CHICKEN

CIRCUIT

COAX

COIL

COMPUTER

CONNECT

COPPER

CURRENT

DATA

ELECTRIC

FENCE

FLEXIBLE

GAUGE

GOLD

HANGER

INSULATED

JEWELRY

LINK

LONG

MESH

METAL

NICKEL

PHONE

POLE

POWER

SHIELDED

SPOOL

STEEL

STRAND

TELEGRAM

THIN

TWIST

VOLTAGE

```
T L D V P M D J P M F G B X
E N A E G U A G O B E N D V
S S E T D N T R W D N S U X
Z T P R E I A N E K C I H C
N R E O R M A T R P E J N X
G A E E O U A R I T P I A C
K N E T L L C R B U C O A O
K D L Y U A S O G K C T C N
Z C D S Y P V H E E W R J N
N O N B D O M L I I L E I E
H I U A L U B O S E W E S C
A L B T C I R T C E L E T T
N W A T X C A B L E N D G K
G G E E H B A R B E D O E U
E U L R I I Y K N I L E H D
R F O Y L O N G Q D E L O P
```

Solution on Page 347

AGENT

AUTO

BILL

BROKER

BUSINESS

CAR

COMPANY

CONTRACT

COST

COVERED

DENTAL

FEES

FIRE

FLOOD

HEALTH

HEDGE

HOME

HOSPITAL

HOUSE

LAW

LEGAL

LIFE

MONEY

PAYMENT

PAYOUT

PET

POLICY

PREMIUM

PROTECT

PROVIDER

QUOTE

RATES

REQUIRED

RISK

SAFETY

SECURITY

TERM

THEFT

TRAVEL

VISION

Solution on Page

```
U S S E R I F L T R A V E L
C A E G D E H C R T E O A K
T F E H T L K Z O P E T O S
H E F D E S U O H M I N E T
C T H M U I M E R P P T C U
L Y T I R U C E S B A A R P
A K L W M G M O S R R E N A
G G A R K O H Q E T Q N M Y
E G E C H S U D N U O V G M
L T H N O O I O I I P P P E
G Y F E T V C R S E D R B N
W C F E O W E I U T O M I T
A I L R P D V R B T O R L I
L L P F L O O D E N T A L I
C O S T Y Z G C E D U C N D
J P A Y O U T Y M M A B F L
```

Solution on Page 347

ANTIQUE

ART

BEAD

BRASS

BRIGHT

BULB

CANDLE

CANOPY

CEILING

CHAIN

CLASSIC

CRYSTAL

DECOR

DESIGN

DINING

DROP

ELEGANT

FANCY

FESTOON

FINIAL

FIXTURE

FORMAL

FRENCH

GLASS

HANGING

HOME

HOOP

HOUSE

LAMP

LIGHT

LUXURY

METAL

MINI

OPERA

ORNATE

PRISM

ROOM

ROUND

SILVER

STYLE

```
D F M E S U O H L A T E M M M
T K O Y A N G D C T N T L O
I O B R A S S E D N F A A O
L U E U M M S I R P E N M R
Q P M X H A N G J U S R P Y
O U O U S I L V E R T O F C
A J H L N H F A U R O X M N
A N J G E N E I T H O G I A
G B T N G L N L N S N C R F
T H G I R B Y S E I Y T E G
G I S G Q C Q T L G A R E D
T E M N H U C I S S A L C R
D B E A D X E S E Y D N V O
M D I H S C A F I N I M T P
D N U O R L B C A N O P Y D
N T L I G H T C B U L B A A
```

Solution on Page 347

AIR

BICYCLE

CAR

DEVICE

DIAPHRAGM

ELECTRIC

ENERGY

ENGINE

EQUIPMENT

FLOW

FLUID

FOOT

FUEL

GAS

GRAVITY

HAND

HEAT

HOSE

INFLATE

LIQUID

MACHINE

MOTOR

OIL

PIPE

PLUNGER

POWER

PRESSURE

PRIME

PUSH

SLURRIES

SUCTION

SUMP

TIRE

TOOL

VACUUM

VALVE

VOLUME

WATER

WELL

WINDMILL

```
B D K O P Y F V F U E L O R
K T V N M K K E T A L F N I
Q L X J Q U V Y K I P N D A
F O W E L L N Z M K T I R E
O O K C A O Y D T E A F P L
B T O V I T N E M P I U Q E
P I Y T I I N I H R Y W K C
S E C V W I R R R E W O P T
H U A Y G P A P U S H L O R
S R M N C G P E Y S D F U I
G E E P M L R N G U I F E C
M C C K U S E I R R U L S A
O I D N U T T H E E Q U O R
T V G N C A A C N O I I H G
O E A N A E W A E I L D E O
R D S K V H E M U L O V Y X
```

Solution on Page 348

ADVANCE

BETTER

CHANGE

COMPANY

COMPUTER

CREATE

DEVELOP

DISCOVERY

ECONOMICS

EFFICIENCY

EVOLUTION

EXPERIMENT

FIRST

GOALS

IDEA

IMPROVE

INDUSTRY

INGENUITY

INNOVATE

INTELLECT

INVENT

KNOWLEDGE

LAB

MARKET

METHOD

NEW

PATENT

PROCESS

PRODUCT

PROGRESS

RESEARCH

SCIENCE

SERVICE

SOLUTION

THINKING

```
T N E T A P R O D U C T S T E
E R E I E G D E L W O N K N
C E Z W N X E C N A V D A E
I S R E T U P M O C B I T V
V E F F I C I E N C Y S S N
R A V S S E C O R P R C Y I
E R I I X P A E D I I O T N
S C N F N A O C F M M V I D
L H N O I T U L O V E E U U
A A O E I D E N E M Z R N S
O N V X I T O L C V P Y E T
G G A S E C U H L R E A G R
B E T T E R S L T E E D N Y
S S E R G O R P O E C A I Y
D E V O R P M I Q S M T T H
M A R K E T H I N K I N G E
```

Solution on Page 348

ABSORB

ACRYLIC

BASEBALL

CASUAL

CHRISTMAS

COVER

DRAWER

DRESS

ELASTIC

FABRIC

FEET

FOOT

GARMENT

GYM

HEEL

HOSIERY

KNEE

KNIT

LACE

LAUNDRY

LEG

LOW

MATE

MISSING

PADDED

PAIR

POLYESTER

PUPPET

RUN

SILK

SIZE

SLIPPER

SPORT

TOE

WARM

WEAR

WOOL

WORK

WOVEN

YARN

Socks

```
K V E L A S T I C J Q M J G
V R E E G A P H N Z F L E O
V E E G Y M R A W O O R Y I
H E A T C I L Y R C A N R C
G N I S S I M R E W A R D K
W K O T N E M R A G Y A N B
M V M D R T Y L J F R Y U J
S A B E L O L L A B E S A B
S K G D G O P A O U I E L R
E L C D P F W S C P S O T O
R I I A U C F W O E O A X S
D S R P P O O S T W H L C B
R V B T P V P A I R H T W A
N R A I E E M M N Z A O A T
P A F N T R R A H U E E E C
Y U M K E M L V P K R O W R
```

Solution on Page 348

AIR

AVIAN

BIRD

BREEDING

CHICKS

CURRENT

DIVING

DRAG

DUCKS

EAGLE

FEATHER

FEEDING

FLY

GEESE

GLIDE

GRACEFUL

GROUP

HEIGHT

HIGH

HOVER

LANDING

LEADER

LIFT

LIGHT

MIGRATE

MUSCLES

NATURE

NORTH

PATTERN

REST

SEASON

SKY

SOAR

SOUTH

SPEED

SWOOP

TRAVEL

VIEW

WEIGHT

WIND

Bird Flight

```
D F F J M X K C O N U X A B
I J E N H I G H O V E R K I
V I E A A J E L E A D E R O
I W D L T T I C H I C K S P
N A I V A H U U L I G H T I
G F N R R R E R G G T H X N
T N G E N L S R E R S X T C
J I I W J P A E O O E K W E
M Y R D E C A N T R A V E L
U A L E E I D T D H S T I G
S F D F P E V Q T I O D G A
C K U Y G O R U Z E N A H E
L L C Z L R O B T I R G T S
E N S U I S O W W D I N O E
S B I R D X K U S L A A A E
V D T S E R Y Y P E R L Y G
```

Solution on Page 348

ASCII

AUTOMATE

BAY

BIT

BYTE

CABLE

CACHE

COPY

CPU

DELETE

DISPLAY

DSL

DVD

ENTER

ERROR

ESCAPE

FAX

FILE

GIF

HELP

HTML

LAPTOP

LASER

MEMORY

MODEM

MONITOR

OPTIONS

PASTE

PIXEL

PRINTER

RAM

SCANNER

SCSI

SERVER

SUPPORT

TOOLS

URL

UTILITY

WEB

WWW

```
B X C D D G Y R O M E M U T
U D V H L Q Q K P T G Y T E
L E E E P R I N T E R L I P
P L X M S U N B I T M E L P
P I A V J P U I O O R S I B
P F F C S C A N N E R C T S
A J Y G D V D I S P L A Y Q
S U P P O R T W D E U P A L
T G W Z O O G Y P T R E B E
E O M A R C Y R O E F V L V
W W W M O D E M T L A S E R
B S L E L B A C P E D R H R
L Y M Q B T S F A D R C C X
R E T N E F C S L O O T A Q
U O H E Y I I P R R I S C S
K I B U Y M I G S S J W K K
```

Solution on Page 349

ACTOR	MUSIC
ADVERTISE	PAPER
ART	PHOTO
BAND	PLAY
CAMPAIGN	PROTEST
CHEAP	ROLL
COLOR	SCHOOL
CONCERT	SIGN
CUSTOM	SPORTS
DORM	STUDENT
EVENT	STYLE
FAMOUS	TAPE
FILM	TEENAGER
FLAT	TEXT
FRAME	TRAVEL
GRAPHIC	TUBE
HANG	WALL
INK	WANTED
MATTED	
MESSAGE	
MODELS	
MOVIE	

```
C S A O A E X H U O T O H P
B B Z C Y V S S P O R T S A
G S T U D E N T S E T O R P
W O R R M N Y F G S T Y L E
R N A O A T K A S L L A W R
T G V E J R N M L C I S U M
X I E S D E I O E P H L V M
E S L I E C R U D I Y O E F
T X M T T N P S O D Q S O I
Z X O R N O Q W M N S G Y L
F E T E A C I H P A R G L M
I T S V W F M G B T H P S
Z X U D R N L E B U T T A V
Q G C A M P A I G N A H E O
Q B M R O D T E G P O W H D
R E P A T P B Z R O L O C E
```

Solution on Page 349

ALLERGY

ALMOND

BAKING

BEECH

BOTANY

BRAZIL

CAN

CHESTNUT

CHRISTMAS

COOK

CORN

CRACK

CRUNCH

CUISINE

CULINARY

DESSERT

EAT

EDIBLE

FILBERT

FOOD

FRUIT

HARD

HAZEL

KERNEL

LEGUME

MIXED

NUTRIENT

NUTRITION

OAK

PARTY

PLANT

PROTEIN

SALT

SEED

SHELL

SNACK

SQUIRREL

TREE

VITAMINS

WALNUT

```
S W Y T R A P C O R N I D Z
H T A V C R L A R Y P A L S
E D V L O U Y N G U D T E N
L S M T N E I R T U N T Z A
L N E P E U E S A D U C A C
E I U R L L T C I N A S H K
N M T T L A D G T N I L D C
R A O A R R N S R L E L Y A
E T H A A I E T Q R A N U R
K I C H K H T T R Z A S H C
N V Y A C H R I S T M A S B
S A B T A E U C O O K W V R
F O O D S Q E B D N O M L A
D E E S S O Q B M I X E D Z
T R E B L I F R U I T K D I
E D I B L E G U M E M V E L
```

Solution on Page 349

ACTOR

AISLE

ARENA

ARTS

AUDIENCE

BALCONY

BOXES

BUILDING

CINEMA

CONCERT

COSTUMES

CREW

CURTAIN

DANCING

DARKNESS

DIRECTOR

DOOR

DRAMA

ENTRANCE

EVENT

EXIT

FILM

LIGHTS

MOVIE

MUSIC

OPERA

PERFORM

PLAY

POPCORN

ROW

SCENERY

SET

SHOW

SINGING

SOUND

STAGE

TICKET

USHER

WALLS

WINGS

At the Theater

```
U F U L I G H T S G S E T A
D N S M U S I C N E E G M D
T N H O G X E I Y A M A R D
I Y E E U N C A N A O T O J
C A R D E N I U O M V S F C
K L N R A A D D C E I N R S
E P Y D A R X I L N E E E I
T N I C D E K E A I W M P N
S R T T E N A N B C U T F G
T O R R N A S C E T E B A I
R C E E A E W E S S C S R N
A P C J D N V O A I S L E G
O O N R O T C E R I D L P M
T P O W O H S E X O B A O L
Q L C U R T A I N I U W B I
J S E H S G N I W C T J F F
```

Solution on Page 349

ACTIVITY

APIARY

ARTIFICIAL

BEE

BOXES

BROOD

BUSY

BUZZING

CELLS

CLAY

CLUSTER

COLONY

COMB

CROPS

DRONE

EGGS

ENCLOSED

FLOWERS

HABITAT

HEXAGON

HONEY

HUM

KEEPER

LARVAE

MUD

NATURAL

NEST

ORDER

POLLEN

PRODUCTION

PROPOLIS

PUPAE

QUEEN

SMOKE

STING

STRUCTURE

SWEET

TREE

WAX

WORKER

```
S Z P T R E E M I Q U E E N
B C B Y D E S O L C N E E O
E R H L W N T I W P F L A B
G O O W A O R D E R L Z M R
G P L O X I U Y N O L O C H
S S A R D T C N P P C S L W
G W R K U C T I Q O M Y A H
N E U E M U U T F L T H Y A
I E T R W D R G N I Z Z U B
T T A S I O E E V S T M X I
S A N M D R L I P X T R E T
M Y P R M P T F I E S C A A
O E O I L C L U S T E R P T
K N O G A X E H N L X K U S
E O E A V R A L L V O R P E
V H U M F I Y S U B B E E N
```

Solution on Page 350

AIR WRENCH

AUTOMOBILE

CHASSIS

CHECKERED FLAG

CIRCUIT

CONCESSIONS

COURSE

CREW CHIEF

DASH

DODGE

DRAG

DRIVER

ENGINE

FINISH LINE

FUEL

GARAGE

GRANDSTAND

GREEN FLAG

HELMET

INFIELD

LAPS

MECHANIC

MOTOR

NASCAR

OVAL

PACE CAR

PASS

PIT CREW

PIT ROAD

POLE

RADIO

SPEEDWAY

SPONSOR

STOCK CAR

TIRES

TRACK

TURN

YELLOW FLAG

```
E O W E L O P I T R O A D D
G R V S D R I V E R M N E O
A O G A P L A S X E A S N D
R S P A L E R C C T T S G G
A N I C L U E H S O T A I E
G O G S O F A D C A L P N L
S P A C S N N K W F N I E I
F S L I I A C E D A L T L B
E Z F C R A H E E H Y C D O
I M W G R W R C S R H R L M
H N O T S E R I T S G E E O
C R L T K C N E A F I W I T
W U L C O I Z D N G A O F U
E T E Q F R A C E C A P N A
R H Y Z A T E M L E H R I S
C I R C U I T O I D A R D Q
```

Solution on Page 350

ANTHRACITE

ASH

BLACK

BURN

CARBON

CINDER

COMBUST

COMMODITY

DEPOSITS

DUST

ELECTRICITY

ENERGY

ENVIRONMENT

FIRE

FOSSIL

FUEL

FURNACE

GRAPHITE

HARD

HEAT

HYDROGEN

LIGNITE

LUMP

MINE

NITROGEN

OXYGEN

PEAT

PETROLEUM

PLANT

POLLUTION

POWER

REFINED

RESOURCE

SHAFT

SMOKE

STEAM

STOCKING

SULFUR

TRAIN

UNDERGROUND

```
Y C I N D E R E S O U R C E
T L E U F G P L N O B R A C
I N M D N S T E A M H E P A
D O E O R D A C A Y I G O N
O I L M S A E T D T L N W R
M T P A N T H R A C I T E U
M U R L L O O I G T S H R F
O L E M A G R C N R S P L L
C L F L E N B I K A O M I U
O O I N O T T T V I F U G S
M P N G S R Y Y J N N L N T
B B E U O G T F I R E G I D
U U D G R X D E P O S I T S
S R E E E T I H P A R G E P
T N N E G Y X O B L A C K B
J E M S H A F T S M O K E T
```

ACCOUNTS

ASSETS

AUDIT

BANK

BARTER

BONDS

BUY

CAPITAL

COSTS

CREDIT

CURRENCY

DEBT

DEMAND

DIVIDEND

DOLLAR

EARNINGS

EQUITY

EXCHANGE

EXPENSES

EXPORT

FEDERAL

IMPORT

INCOME

IRS

LABOR

LOAN

LOSS

MARGIN

MARKET

NET

PAYABLE

PROFIT

REFUND

REPORT

REVENUE

SALES

STOCKS

SUPPLY

TAXES

TRADE

Business Economics

```
Q T S M K D I S U P P L Y J
E E M O C N I S T S O C R P
Z K E G N A H C X E S U E T
K R A D I M P O R T S T T B
V A R I G E Z I O E R S R E
Y M N V R D L C T O P O A D
S C I I A L K A P A I O B A
S L N D M S A X R V L T R R
O U G E X P E N S E S I P T
L Y S N R R A L L O D D R I
Z O T D E R T Y Y P S E O D
B U A I R B U L A B O R F U
O S T N U O C C A B A C I A
N J Z Y O Q A T W T L N T W
D N U F E R E V E N U E K R
S A L E S E X A T E N C I D
```

Solution on Page 350

AXLE	MOTOR
BIKE	PARKING
BRAKE	POPULAR
CHEAP	RIDE
CHOPPER	ROAD
CITY	SADDLE
CYCLE	SAFE
DELIVERY	SEAT
DRIVE	SMALL
EASY	SPEED
ENGINE	STORAGE
EUROPE	STREET
FAST	TIRES
GAS	TRAVEL
HARLEY	VEHICLE
HELMET	VESPA
HIGHWAY	WHEEL
HONDA	WIND
ITALY	
LICENSE	
LIGHTS	
MOPED	

```
J S V F C D W Y X I Y L F G
Z M W K L N T H T S A F N K
K E O E W I B R A K E I Y V
O H E P C W F E T P K L S Z
D H E L E H S T O R A G E Q
W P W L D D O R A T A V A V
N T C E M D U P I Y I V T A
G Y E C H E A P P R Z F E X
C P L I G H T S D E K I B L
S Y Z M O T O R I V R U E E
S R E N Y A W H G I H S N J
G O D L L A M S N L N N G T
G A S R R S T R E E T F I P
W D Z E F A S R C D D R N H
A P S E V E H I C L E I E Y
O L P O P U L A R S C G R K
```

Solution on Page 351

ADOPTION

AQUARIUM

BIRD

BREEDER

CAGE

CARE

CATS

COLLAR

DOGS

ENJOYMENT

EXOTIC

FAMILY

FERRET

FROG

FUR

GERBIL

GOLDFISH

HAMSTER

HORSE

KITTENS

LITTER

LIZARD

LOVE

LOYAL

MEDICINE

NEUTER

OWNER

PARAKEET

PARROT

PET FOOD

PUPPY

RABBITS

REPTILES

SNAKES

SPAY

STORE

TRAINING

TURTLE

WALK

WATER

```
B M J T F Y P P U P C C P L
S E K A N S R B L H I A A O
K D L A G T E L I T T E R V
D I A D I A D H O R S E R E
P C W O F C E X T Y S G O D
E I Y P A R E T S M A H T T
T N R T M U R E P T I L E S
F E J I I F B S T O R E G N
O N G O L D F I S H K A A E
O E N N Y C O L L A R B C T
D U I W A M U I R A U Q A T
I T N B P H E A G O R F E I
X E I O S W P N C W L R F K
J R A B B I T S T N R Q Q H
D D R A Z I L U G E R B I L
E L T R U T Z B F R E T A W
```

Solution on Page 351

Answers

Bread Maker

Outstanding

Office Life

Mexican Cuisine

314

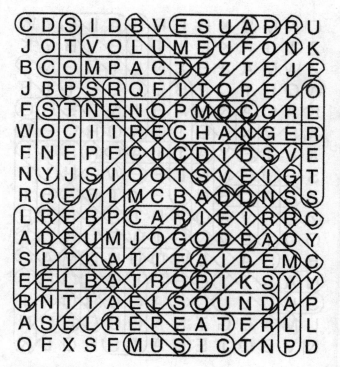

CD Player

Onions

The Mighty Oak

Baggage

Weaving

Pirates at Sea

Desk

Towels

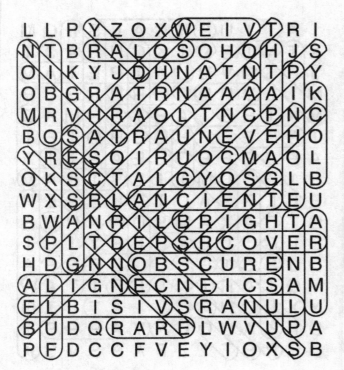

Solar Eclipse

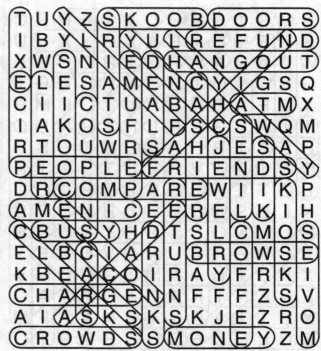

Shopping Complex

Play Tennis

Roots

Biggest Fan

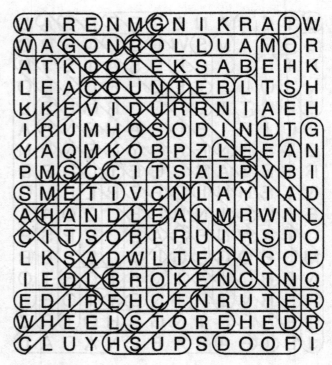

Ironing

Common First Names

Shopping Carts

Pants

Games

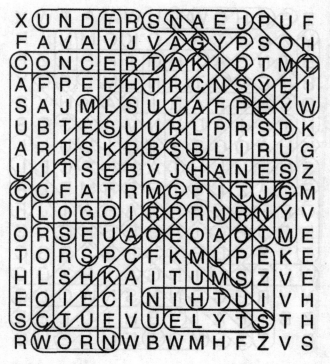

T-Shirts

Shipping Out

Sporting

Silver Screen

Sea Otter

Unicycle

Orbit

Poker Games

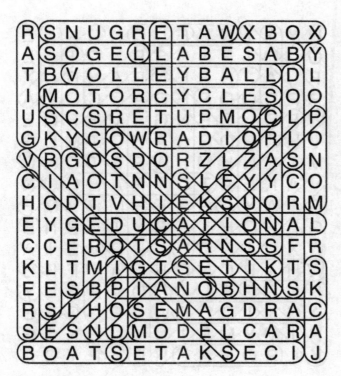

All Kinds of Toys

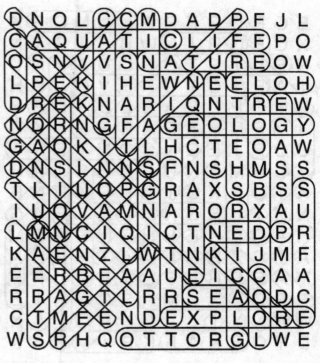

Inside a Cave

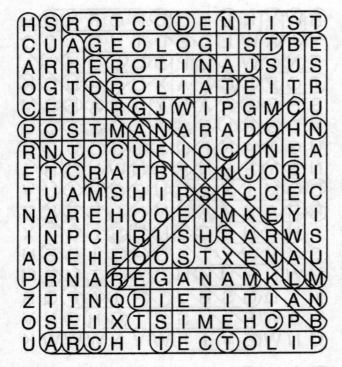

Get a Job

Metal

Smile

Carriage

Tetris

Barrel

Ox

A Day at the Park

Back in the Saddle

Whiteboard

Police Work

Stapler

Down the Aisle

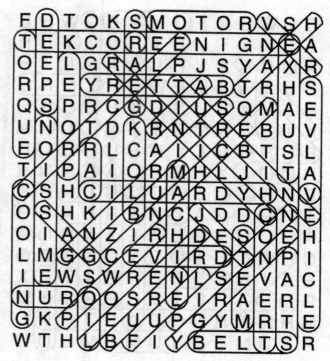

Start Your Engines

Rings

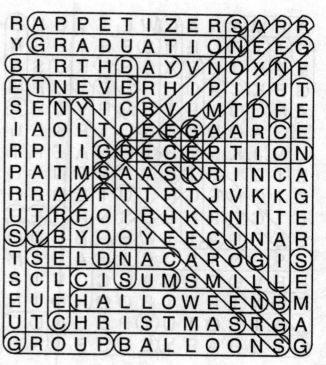

Throw a Party

Ropes

Travel Trailer

Book Lovers

Fun Fair

Vintage Typewriters

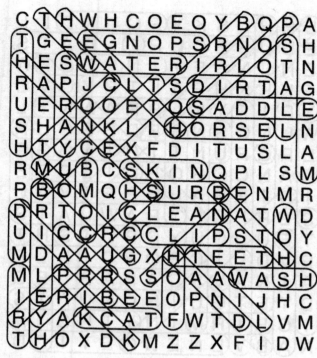

Horse Grooming

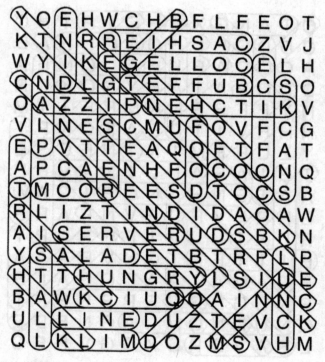

Cafeteria

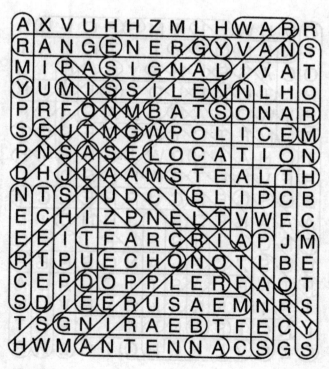

Radar

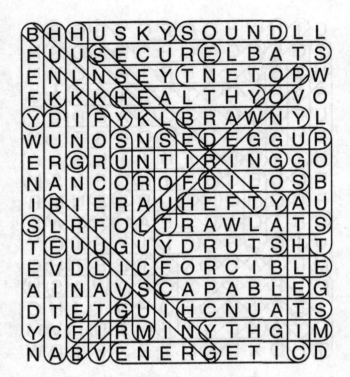

Powerful Words

Around the Reservoir

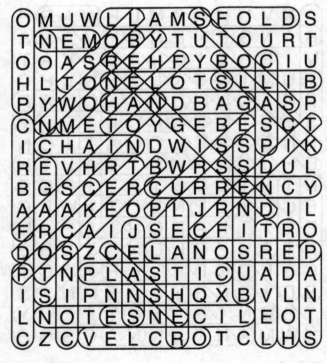

Wallet

Flavor

Christmas Display

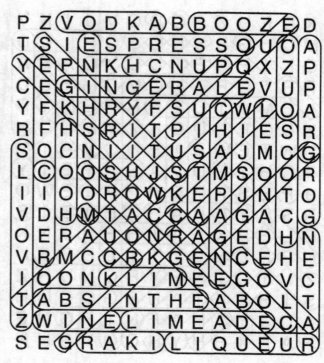

Have a Sip

Electric

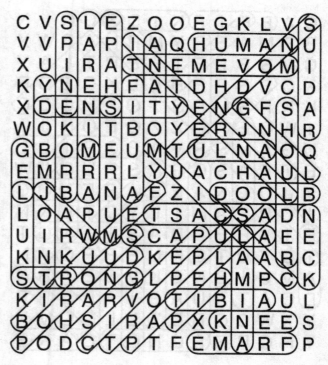

Bone

Baby Words

Investment Jargon

A Perfect Picnic

Sing the Blues

330

School Time

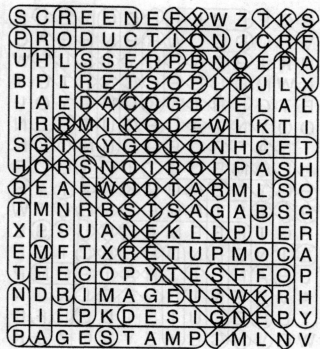

Printing

Titanium

Part of Your Car

Chimney

Lighthouse

Nails

Ice Cream, Please

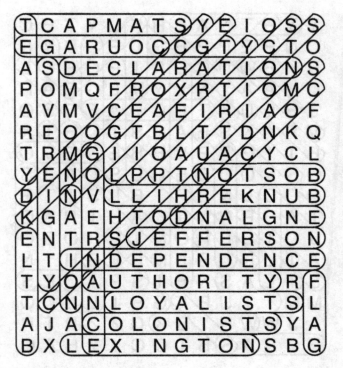

Revolutionary

The Western Frontier

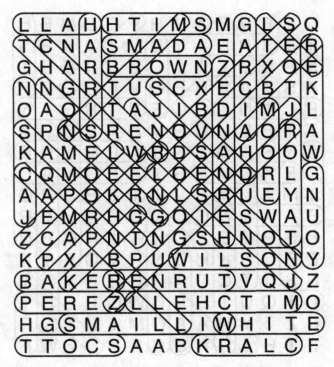

Common Family Names

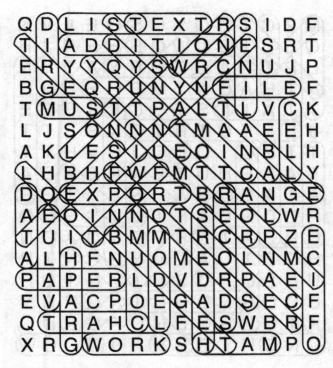

Spreadsheet

On the Map

The Kitchen

Lathes

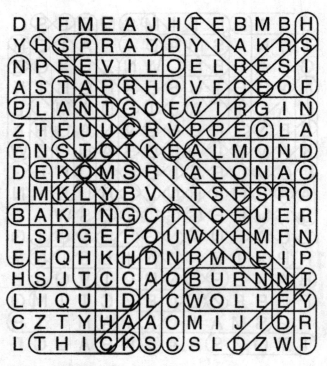

Cooking Oil

Cardboard

Spoons

I H S T U O C S T N E T B N W
T J E A H L A E N X S S I E
A S U K T A S I H A O N V Q
E L N D A N R S S C T O O F
R A O I P T H T K E T U H W
T M G J A E S S R S L A R P
E I A L L R I U T O M O M E
R N G T O N E E M M P W P S
B A E F S V H H O M M E E Z
O R F E O C E C T S E H G G
O Y C T T H K S O A T R N L
T T A A I N C Q Z O E I T O L O G
S F H X Y N A N L L K W K G
Y C L L I R G C O I J I T S
W O O D S I N O H P E D N O
R S T F A R C A B I N F F G

Go Camping

W V W K K P H A S E N O T S
I N D N U O R G C S U D M P
V R N E R I G I D C A I H U
K C O R T O U G H I N L C J
C L M N F I R M G E U O G D
O P A Q U E N F R N N Q O V
L Q I I C U C A R C Y O I O
B F D G R O L Y R E W M I L
Q F I L L E D E T G T A A U
T R X O C R T S N N T T O M
D E R S U E S A E O E B A E
M E X T U A S Z M M J C W M
V Z S A M T O S E E S N E D
N E O T E R P A C K E D A R
I J Z E F N O T H G I E W A H
N D L O G W V F E T E M T H

Solid

Middle Eastern Cuisine

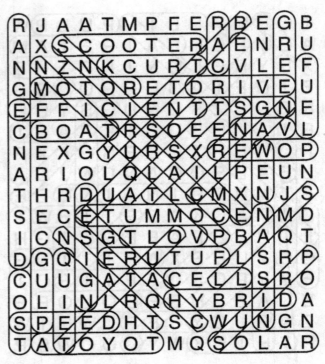

Electric Vehicles

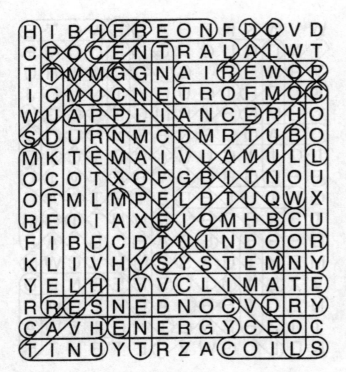

Air Conditioning

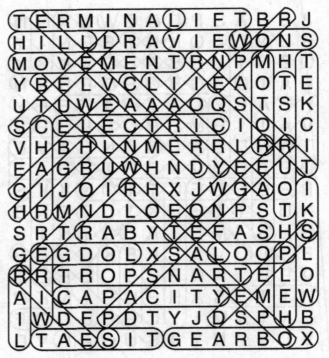

Chairlift

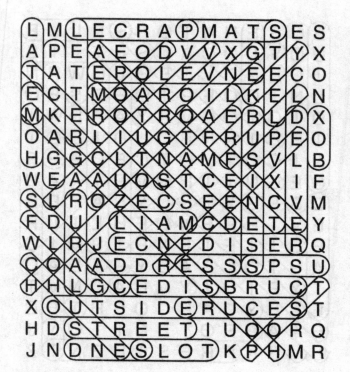

Mailbox

Collars

Straw

Nail Polish

Have a Beer

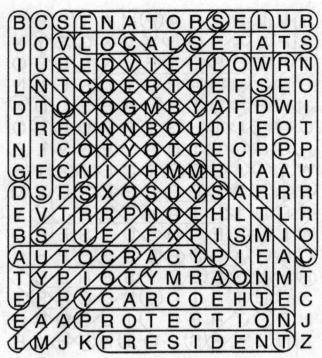

The Government

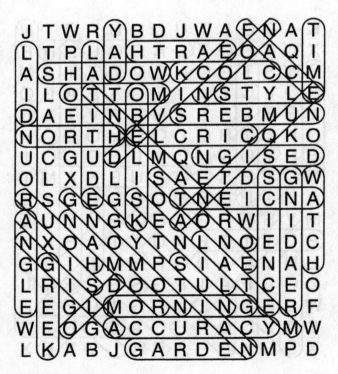

Sundial

Cream

Renewable Energy

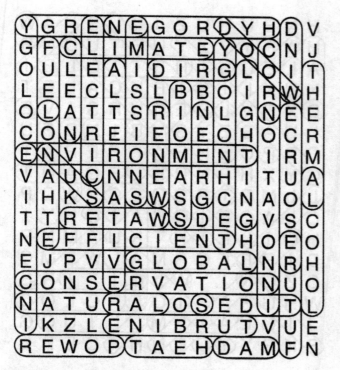

Summer Fun

Radio-Controlled Aircraft

Carousel

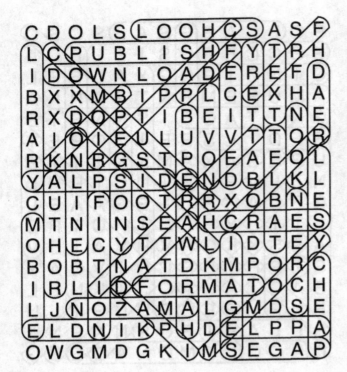

E-Books

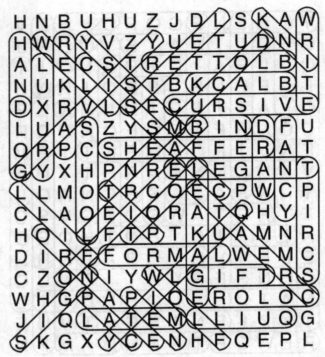

Fountain Pens

Irrigation

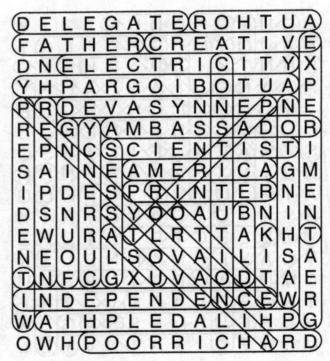

Ben Franklin

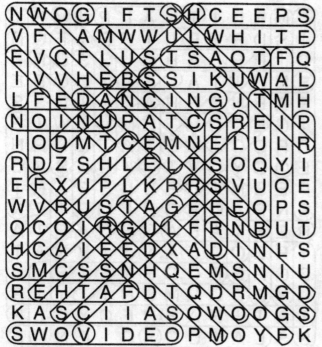

Wedding Day

Plenty of Time

Property

Little Gifts

Electronic Games

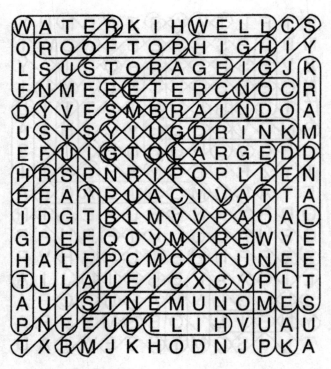

Ecology

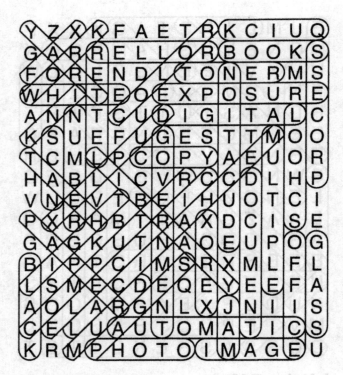

Photocopier

Water Tower

Staying Fit

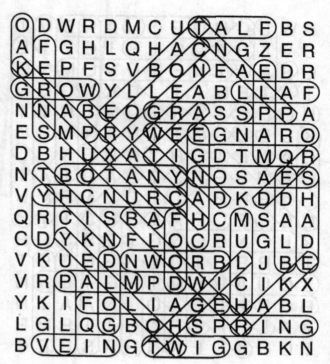

Leaves

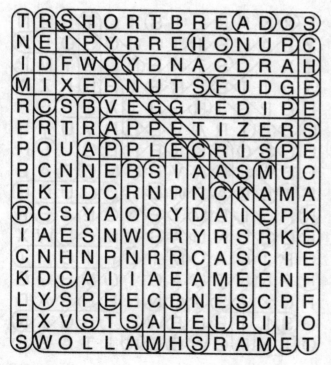

Tasty

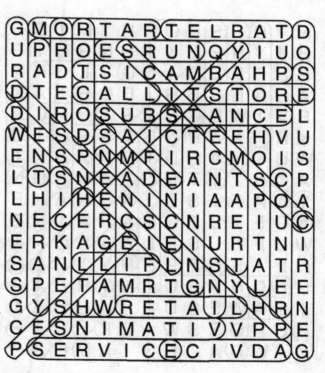

Pharmacy

Clock Tower

Street Smart

Recycle

Pillow

Stadium

Waterfall

Testing, Testing

Cute as a Button

Firefighting

Lots of Friends

At the Grocery

Sink

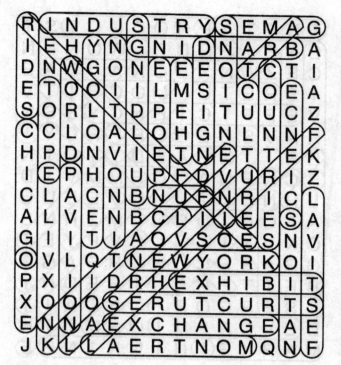

World Expo

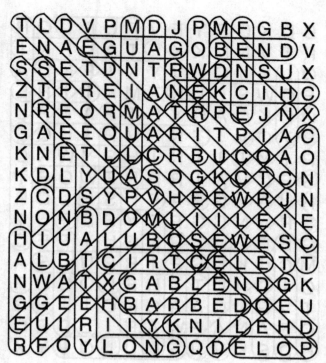

Wire

Insurance

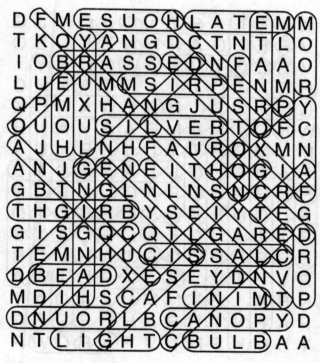

Chandelier

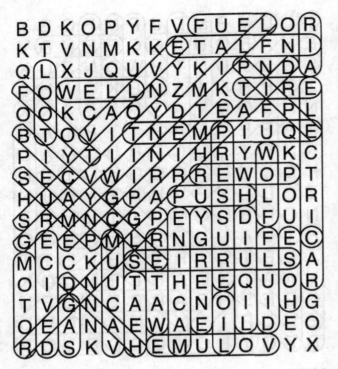

Pump

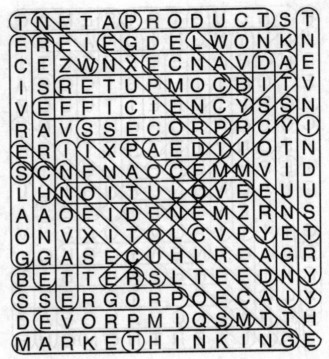

Innovation

Socks

Bird Flight

Computer Terms

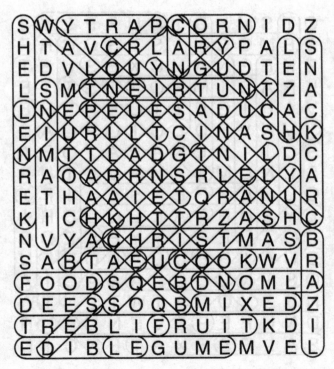

Go Nuts

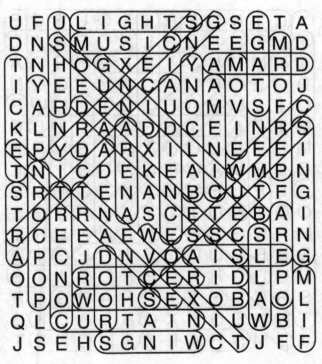

Poster

At the Theater

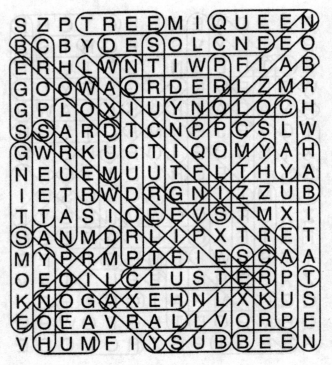

Beehive

Racing

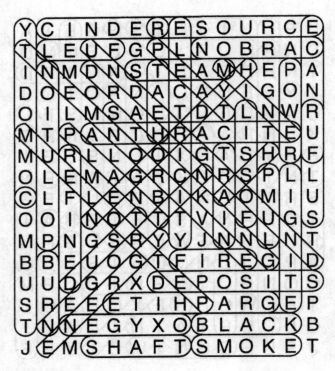

Coal

Business Economics

Scooters

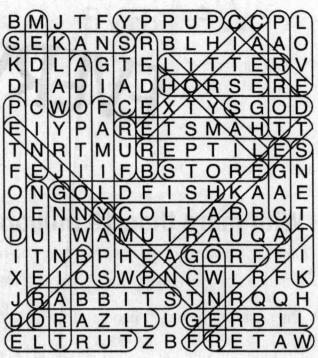

Pet Friends

We Have
EVERYTHING®
on Anything!

With more than 19 million copies sold, the Everything® series has become one of America's favorite resources for solving problems, learning new skills, and organizing lives. Our brand is not only recognizable—it's also welcomed.

The series is a hand-in-hand partner for people who are ready to tackle new subjects—like you!

For more information on the Everything® series, please visit *www.adamsmedia.com.*

The Everything® list spans a wide range of subjects, with more than 500 titles covering 25 different categories:

Business	History	Reference
Careers	Home Improvement	Religion
Children's Storybooks	Everything Kids	Self-Help
Computers	Languages	Sports & Fitness
Cooking	Music	Travel
Crafts and Hobbies	New Age	Wedding
Education/Schools	Parenting	Writing
Games and Puzzles	Personal Finance	
Health	Pets	